Making Science Accessible to English Learners

A Guidebook for Teachers

UPDATED EDITION

John Carr, Ursula Sexton, & Rachel Lagunoff

ISBN: 978-0-914409-40-3

Library of Congress Control Number: 2007936479

This book is printed on recycled paper. The cover contains 50% recycled content, and the text contains 15% recycled content.

WestEd, a national nonpartisan, nonprofit research, development, and service agency, works with education and other communities to promote excellence, achieve equity, and improve learning for children, youth, and adults. WestEd has 16 offices nationwide, from Washington and Boston to Arizona and California. Its corporate headquarters are in San Francisco.

WestEd books and products are available throughout many bookstores. To contact WestEd directly, call our Publication Center at 1-888-293-7833.

For more information about WestEd:

Visit www.WestEd.org

Call 415-565-3000 or toll free 877-4-WestEd

Write WestEd

730 Harrison Street
San Francisco, CA 94107-1242

Contents

Figures

Tools and Strategies

Preface

We developed this guidebook for middle and high school science teachers who are looking for practical ways to help English learners in their classrooms understand the rigorous science content reflected in state standards. Science teachers at the elementary school level should also find the strategies in this guidebook relevant and useful, although the content of specific examples will not always reflect elementary school standards.

The guidebook is meant for use in conjunction with district textbooks and other district materials and within a district program of teacher support that includes professional development, collegial discussions, and coaching. It is our hope that teachers will have embedded opportunities to practice the strategies described here, discuss them, observe one another, and become increasingly facile choosing and combining strategies within lesson plans and spontaneously, whenever opportunities arise. Because this kind of learning develops over time, we urge districts to make available the ongoing time and support necessary for successful appropriation and implementation.

Thank you to the persistent content area teachers who prodded us over several years to create resources for teaching content area subjects to English learners. We can only hope this is the kind of resource they had in mind.

We were very fortunate to have had the advice of a number of experts in science instruction and the instruction of English learners. Their generosity in reviewing the manuscript led to the current form of the guidebook and to many refinements in its execution. We are extremely grateful for the benefit of their expertise.

Veronica Aquila, California Department of Education
Dolores Beltran, California State University, Los Angeles
Diane Carnahan, Regional Director, K–12 Alliance at WestEd
Cindy Davis-Harris, Grossmont (CA) Union High School District
Fred Dobb, California Department of Education
Joya Deutsch, 49ers Academy, Ravenswood (CA) School District
Paula Jacobs, California Department of Education
Sonia Jaramilla-Perez, LASERS Rural Schools, Alisal (CA) School District
Phil Lafontaine, California Department of Education
Zaida McCall-Perez, Hayward (CA) Unified School District
William Pence, California High School, San Ramon (CA) Unified School District
Christopher Vang, California State University, Stanislaus
Yee Wan, Santa Clara (CA) County Office of Education

REMARKS ON THE UPDATED EDITION

This updated edition features a new, larger, and easy-to-read format. Additional content grew out of our work in the spring of 2007 with Dr. Todd Ullah, Elizabeth Garcia, and the secondary science leadership cadre in the Los Angeles Unified School District (LAUSD) Science Branch.

In Chapter 4, we simplify the steps in the Teaching Vocabulary section, making it easier for science teachers to identify and introduce important new terms. We emphasize the idea that many new words and phrases are best taught during the main part of a lesson as students explore and explain new concepts. Some new words may be introduced at the start of a lesson or just before reading the texts.

In Chapter 5, we provide answers to two important questions that arose in feedback we received from the original volume. Many teachers asked how to help students read the textbook, especially English learners and other struggling readers. In response, we expand on how to plan instruction so that students at different reading levels can access textbooks and other texts. Secondly, many teachers new to differentiating instruction for English learners asked about a viable way to plan a lesson. To answer this question, we offer the "big ideas" for integrating strategies and thereby differentiating instruction, and then provide an example of a fairly simple lesson plan that would cover a few days, and perhaps an entire unit.

We welcome your feedback as well; please write to us at info@WestEd.org, or contact us through www.WestEd.org.

Introduction

Every classroom has students with diverse learning needs and interests, and this diversity is increasing as more English learners enter our education system. English learners are themselves quite diverse — in their native language, level of English language development, prior experiences, and formal education. Like other students, English learners may prefer particular learning modalities and styles, may be designated for special education services, or may have an innate bent for science. Since no single method works for all students, effective teachers continually explore and experiment with new ways to engage all students in successful learning. They learn to "differentiate" instruction to meet students "where they are" and to help them all achieve the same set of standards.

Teaching a rigorous science curriculum in ways that ensure English learners can understand the content and demonstrate what they have learned is challenging, but it is certainly possible. This guidebook provides practical tools and strategies that allow science teachers to help their English learners think like scientists, express themselves as scientists, and develop the skills and confidence to become scientists.

For all students, a large part of learning science is learning the language of science and using science terminology meaningfully within academic conversations and written work. Understandably, science students who are simultaneously learning the English language need extra support. On the other hand, science is a fitting content area for the instructional approach that works best for English learners — hands-on and inquiry-based instruction. This guidebook addresses the language aspects of science instruction with concrete tools and strategies and tries as well to capitalize on the visual and experiential aspects of science that are such a boon to English learners.

For teachers who have participated in professional development related to working with English learners or who have read professional books and articles about best practices for teaching and assessing English learners, we expect that many of the ideas presented here are somewhat familiar. We have pulled together the best ideas, tools, and strategies from a variety of sources; presented them in a practical, succinct format; and pointed out their interconnections. For the purposes of designing this guidebook, we have assumed that the teacher is monolingual in English, has no bilingual classroom aides, and has English learner students who may represent two or more non-English native languages. Our approach to teaching English learners is similar to popular models such as CALLA[1] and SIOP.[2] The guidebook also has close fidelity with the ideas in the National Science Teachers Association's publication, *Science for English Language Learners*,[3] to which our coauthor, Ursula Sexton, contributed.

While effective science teachers are also language teachers, most science teachers may not have had extensive training in the pedagogy of English language arts or in English language development (ELD).

Ideally, the responsibility in a school for effectively teaching English learners is shared among teachers who recognize ways to coordinate English development across subject areas. We urge science teachers to collaborate with English and ELD teachers to build the academic language of the English learners they share. The English and ELD teachers can offer teaching suggestions, insights about particular students, and instructional help with specific skills, such as note taking or report writing, that English learners must master in conjunction with science assignments.

Finally, we encourage all teachers in a school to work together to provide a uniform, consistent instructional approach with core instructional strategies. Truly effective instruction that results in proficient high school graduates is a long-term, schoolwide, team effort.

ENDNOTES FOR INTRODUCTION

[1] Chamot, A.U., & O'Malley, J.M. (1994). *The CALLA handbook: Implementing the cognitive academic language learning approach.* Reading, MA: Addison-Wesley.

[2] Echevarria, J., Vogt, M., & Short, D.J. (2004). *Making content comprehensible for English learners: The SIOP model* (2nd ed.). San Francisco: Pearson Education.

[3] Fathman, A.K., & Crowther, D.T. (Eds.) (2005). *Science for English language learners: K–12 classroom strategies.* Arlington, VA: National Science Teachers Association.

CHAPTER 1
Teaching Science

This chapter offers an overview of science pedagogy applied to English learners, beginning with principles of learning and motivation that apply to all learners. We review the 5 Es instructional model proposed over a decade ago by Roger W. Bybee[1] not only because it is widely respected, but especially because its highly contextualized format allows students to participate fully even though they may be at different levels of science and English literacy. Along with the 5 Es approach, we discuss how three common modes of teaching can benefit English learners, and we introduce the first of many specific strategies to differentiate science instruction for English learners.

PRINCIPLES OF LEARNING AND MOTIVATION

Regardless of whether students are native English speakers or English learners, three research-based principles about how people learn[2] guide effective science teaching and learning. These principles are the foundation of all of the ideas and strategies presented in this guidebook. Making science accessible to English learners means, first of all, recognizing how any student learns.

Principle 1. Students come to the classroom with preconceptions about how the world works. If their initial understanding is not engaged, they may fail to grasp the new concepts and information that are taught, or they may learn them for purposes of a test but revert to their preconceptions outside the classroom.

English learners, like any learners, need a way to connect what they know with what they need to learn.

Principle 2. To develop competence in an area of inquiry, students must (a) have a deep foundation of factual knowledge, (b) understand facts and ideas in the context of a conceptual framework, and (c) organize knowledge in ways that facilitate retrieval and application.

English learners, like any learners, need to learn facts and ideas and need to be able to relate and organize them conceptually.

Principle 3. A metacognitive approach to instruction can help students learn to take control of their own learning by defining learning goals and monitoring their progress in achieving them.

English learners, like any learners, benefit from reflecting on their learning goals and progress. English learners, unlike native English speakers, will need to apply a metacognitive approach to learning English as well as to learning discipline-specific content — in this case, science content.

The artful teacher brings these principles to life for each student, recognizing a student's current level of knowledge and understanding and facilitating each student's growth as a self-directed learner. A respectful classroom climate is key to a teacher's success in being able to do this. Often a visitor can step into a classroom and feel a distinct climate, whether of respect and caring, fear of ridicule, or boredom and detachment. A positive climate is established by teacher modeling and facilitation and is sustained by student practice.

In a safe learning community, because students are patient with one another and do not laugh at mistakes, they can all relax. With their anxiety lowered, students are physiologically more able to accept new challenges and grapple with new concepts and problems.[3] Because English learners can be expected to feel high levels of anxiety about all the challenges they face, it is especially important for them to feel respected by the teacher and other students, whether they are struggling to learn English and science or to communicate different cultural and religious perspectives they may bring to discussions.

Within inclusive classrooms, educators increasingly recognize that equal and equitable are not synonymous.[4] Widespread interest in differentiating instruction reflects the understanding that students learn in different ways, but they do learn. Providing a high-quality science education for all students means planning and using strategies that fit diverse students.

THE 5 Es MODEL OF TEACHING AND LEARNING SCIENCE

The 5 Es model represents a recursive cycle of cognitive stages in inquiry-based learning: engage, explore, explain, elaborate, and evaluate. As the arrows in the figure to the right denote, the stages are not necessarily linear; there may well be back and forth progression between stages, especially between explore and explain and between explain and elaborate. The evaluate stage crosses into the other four as students continually reflect on what they do and do not know. Typically, not all five stages would be experienced in a single classroom period, but all five would certainly be embedded in a lesson or unit lasting days or weeks.

Based on constructivist learning theory, the 5 Es approach capitalizes on hands-on activities, students' curiosity, and academic discussion among students. It should be a key part of all students' science education, explicitly connected to target concepts and content standards and used in conjunction with other methods, including direct instruction.

The following descriptors[5] of the 5 E stages are complemented by excerpts from an account[6] of a teacher's vision for implementing each stage in the classroom. Figure 1.1 presents yet another way to understand the 5 Es, with teacher and student roles delineated.

Engage

The teacher starts the learning process by involving students in making connections between their past and present learning experiences. This stage is meant to create interest, generate curiosity, and raise questions and problems, helping students engage in their own learning process while facilitating opportunities for the teacher to identify students' misconceptions. Any activity a teacher might use to engage students should be explicitly connected to content and standards in the unit lesson.

> **In my classroom . . .** I begin my lesson plan with an intriguing idea, image, or question to engage students. I pose questions about what my students already know, and students pose questions about what they want to learn. It alerts me to misconceptions.

Explore

The teacher guides students as they investigate or perform an experiment about a phenomenon and arrive at a common understanding of certain concepts, processes, and skills. The teacher designs activities that encourage students to construct new knowledge or skills, propose preliminary predictions and hypotheses, "puzzle" through problems, and try alternatives to solve a problem.

> **In my classroom . . .** I do not tell students the concepts I want them to eventually know. Instead, I expect them to think critically about the concepts by experimenting, investigating, observing, classifying, communicating, measuring, predicting, and interpreting. This active engagement arouses curiosity and leads students to discover new ideas, confirm prior assumptions, or perhaps challenge their thinking.

Explain

The teacher guides students as they demonstrate or explain their conceptual understanding, process skills, or behaviors. They debate alternative explanations and contrast new facts with prior misconceptions. As appropriate, the teacher directs their attention to aspects of their earlier "engage" and "explore" experiences. Students organize information into evidence-based statements, using the academic language of science.

> **In my classroom . . .** I guide students' thinking by questioning and facilitating peer discussions to arrive at explanations for scientific phenomena. I give students time to think, and I facilitate student–student discussions to correct misconceptions. It is a time to question and justify answers. Students do not just pose questions and I answer, nor do they simply give answers and I decide what is right or wrong.

Elaborate

The teacher monitors activities and facilitates discussions that challenge and extend students' conceptual understanding and skills. Students apply what they learned to new experiences to develop, extend, connect, and deepen their understanding.

> **In my classroom . . .** I help students compare, contrast, combine, synthesize, generalize, and make inferences by introducing a somewhat different context from what they just experienced. I want students to apply new knowledge, make connections, and extend ideas.

FIGURE 1.1. The 5 Es Instructional Model

Purpose	Teacher Role	Student Role
Engage		
To initiate the lesson An engagement activity connects past and present learning experiences, anticipates new ideas, and organizes students' thinking toward standards and outcomes.	» create interest » generate curiosity » raise questions and problems » elicit responses that uncover students' current knowledge about the concept/topic	» ask questions such as "Why did this happen?" "What do I already know about this?" "What can I find out about this?" "How can this problem be solved?" » show interest in the topic
Explore		
To provide students with a common base of experiences within which current concepts, processes, and skills are identified and developed	» guide students to work together without direct instruction » observe and listen to students as they interact » ask probing questions to redirect students' investigations as needed » provide time for students to puzzle through problems » act as a consultant for students	» think creatively within the limits of the activity » test predictions and hypotheses » form new predictions and hypotheses » try alternatives to solve a problem and discuss them with others » record observations and ideas » suspend judgment » test ideas
Explain		
To focus students on a particular aspect of their prior stage experiences This stage provides opportunities for students to demonstrate their conceptual understanding and process skills. This stage may be an opportunity to introduce a concept, process, or skill.	» guide students to explain concepts and definitions in their own words » ask for justification (evidence) and clarification from students » formally provide definitions, explanations, and new vocabulary » use students' previous experiences as the basis for explaining concepts	» explain possible solutions or answers to other students » listen critically to and question respectfully other students' explanations » listen and try to comprehend explanations offered by the teacher » refer to previous activities

FIGURE 1.1. The 5 Es Instructional Model (continued)

Purpose	Teacher Role	Student Role
Elaborate		
To challenge and extend students' conceptual understanding and skills Through new experiences, students develop deeper and broader understanding, more information, and adequate skills.	» expect students to use learned academic language in a new context » encourage students to apply the concepts and skills in new situations » remind students of alternative explanations » refer students to alternative explanations	» apply new labels, definitions, explanations, and skills in new but connected situations » use previous information to ask questions, propose solutions, make decisions, and design experiments » draw reasonable conclusions from evidence » record observations or explanations
Evaluate		
To encourage students to assess their understanding and abilities and to provide opportunities for teachers to evaluate student progress	» refer students to existing data and evidence and ask, "What do you already know?" "Why do you think…?" » observe students as they apply new concepts and skills » assess students' knowledge/skills » look for evidence that students have changed their thinking » ask students to assess their learning and group process skills » ask open-ended questions such as "What evidence do you have?" "What do you know about the problem?"	» check for understanding among peers » answer open-ended questions by using observations, evidence, and previously accepted explanations » demonstrate an understanding or knowledge of the concept or skill » evaluate own progress and knowledge » ask related questions that would encourage future investigations

Source: R.W. Bybee (1997). *Achieving scientific literacy: From purposes to practices.* Portsmouth, NH: Heinemann. Adapted with permission.

Evaluate

The teacher evaluates students' progress and students assess themselves throughout the other stages. Feedback may come from checking for understanding (e.g., with hand gestures, white boards), quizzes, student discussions, or journals, to name a few techniques. The teacher uses the feedback to reflect on the effectiveness of the lesson, making midcourse adjustments as indicated to better fit the needs and interests of students. The students use the feedback to reflect on what they understand and what they still need to learn or want to know next.

> **In my classroom . . .** I test more than factual knowledge; I challenge students to construct ideas and explanations during an assessment. I want students to construct knowledge and build skills during instruction, and I want assessments to reflect my objectives and the content standards.

Throughout the 5 Es cycle, the role of the teacher is multifaceted. As a facilitator, the teacher nurtures creative thinking, problem solving, interaction, communication, and discovery. As a model, the teacher initiates thinking processes, inspires positive attitudes toward learning, motivates, and demonstrates skill-building techniques. Finally, as a guide, the teacher helps to bridge language gaps and foster individuality, collaboration, and personal growth. The teacher flows in and out of these various roles within each lesson, both as planned and as opportunities arise.

Part of this flow can be captured by the three modes of instruction that describe the participatory roles of the teacher and students. How to use these modes in interaction with the 5 Es and to address the special needs of English learners is discussed below. Figure 1.2 is a simple matrix of the most common combinations of the 5 E stages and three modes of instruction.

FIGURE 1.2. **Common Combinations of 5 E Stages and Modes of Instruction**			
	Participatory Mode of Instruction		
5 Es STAGE	**Teacher-Directed**	**Teacher-Assisted**	**Peer-Assisted**
Engage	●		
Explore			●
Explain		●	●
Elaborate		●	●
Evaluate	●	●	●

THREE MODES OF INSTRUCTION APPLIED TO ENGLISH LEARNERS

All teachers commonly mix three modes of instruction — teacher-directed, teacher-assisted, and peer-assisted — throughout their lessons (see figure 1.3). In a science classroom, different modes present different benefits and opportunities for students. For the English learners in a classroom, special considerations can improve the effectiveness of each of these modes.

Teacher-directed. English learners will feel comfortable in teacher-directed instruction when the teacher provides comprehensible input, using language and speech students can understand, supported with visuals and demonstrations.

Teacher-assisted. English learners will feel more comfortable speaking in teacher-assisted conversations when the teacher establishes a risk-free, caring climate and encourages responses at students' level of comprehending input and producing meaningful output.

Peer-assisted. English learners will feel comfortable in peer-assisted instruction when respected and supported by peers in the group and when group tasks are within their communication capabilities. Peer-assisted instruction is an opportunity for English learners to use their native academic language (if grouped by same language) and to participate as English listeners and speakers as key concepts are repeated and rephrased in English during the whole class discussion.

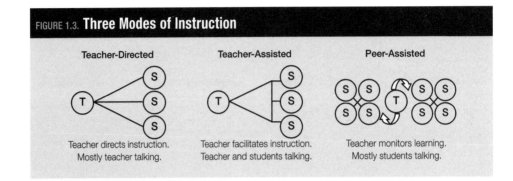

FIGURE 1.3. Three Modes of Instruction

Teacher-Directed	Teacher-Assisted	Peer-Assisted
Teacher directs instruction. Mostly teacher talking.	Teacher facilitates instruction. Teacher and students talking.	Teacher monitors learning. Mostly students talking.

Teacher-Directed Instruction

In teacher-directed instruction, the teacher provides direct instruction to the whole class and individual students respond to the teacher; most interactions are teacher–student. The teacher initiates concept development by giving direct instruction, demonstrating to the whole class, and modeling specific scientific protocols and expected behaviors and processes. The teacher combines saying with showing —supporting oral instruction with pictures, illustrations, realia, graphic organizers, models, demonstrations, video clips, and other visuals. Teacher-directed instruction gives students access to the information they need to begin processing and manipulating ideas, safely use instruments, clarify concepts, and help build connections that facilitate greater understanding of science.

APPLICATIONS FOR ENGLISH LEARNERS

Teacher modeling is an important support for English learners. English learners need to see completed projects and writing assignments; some students may never have had formal schooling or participated in similar tasks in their former countries. Also, before students engage in teacher-assisted discussions and peer-assisted learning activities, the teacher needs to model expected social behaviors and procedures.

When speaking, the teacher can target the listening abilities of English learners in terms of enunciation, speed, intonation, and use of vocabulary, idioms, and contractions. With English learners who are at novice levels, simple subject-verb-object sentences free of idioms and colloquial expressions are necessary. (It can be surprising how many expressions such as "no way," or "make up your mind," or even "take a seat" pepper typical classroom instruction, to the befuddlement of English learners.)

For the benefit of English learners as well as other students, all teacher-directed interactions should be divided into chunks no longer than 15 minutes. Students need time to process each chunk before encountering another chunk.[7] This processing involves relating new information to prior knowledge and experiences, confronting any prior misunderstandings, and constructing new understandings. English learners may also need extra time to listen in English, think in their primary language, and translate their thinking back into English. In some instances they may also want to discuss unknown English vocabulary and new science concepts with another speaker of their primary language.

Between chunks of presented material and information, the teacher checks for understanding. Research indicates that learning improves for the whole class and the achievement gap narrows when the teacher uses techniques to get feedback about each student's understanding during direct instruction and immediately makes appropriate adjustments.[8]

Calling on individual students is a way to collect feedback from a few students at a time. Alternative ways to check for understanding can provide broader information and encourage all students to respond:

>> Students use white boards to write and display short answers.

>> Students signal agreement/disagreement/confusion with a point of view, solution, or approach using colored cards or hand gestures.

>> Students answer chorally.

>> Students work in teams to respond. For example, teams contribute to a collective class solution to a problem; partners talk with one another in English or their primary language before reporting to the class in English.

When asking a question of the whole class, the teacher waits several seconds so that all students have ample opportunity to process the question and think about an answer (three to seven seconds depending on the difficulty of the question). The teacher may acknowledge early "hand raisers" with a nod while still waiting to give everyone time to think of an answer. Wait time allows English learners to decipher the question, think, and formulate an answer in English. It also encourages more students to respond. To resist the urge to keep the lesson pace moving rapidly, the teacher may use a technique such as counting silently or pacing the floor one step per second. When students are called on, walking close to the student being questioned may lessen the student's anxiety about speaking in front of many peers. For English learners, hearing other students rephrase information provides additional opportunities to learn science vocabulary and comprehend important ideas.

Teacher-Assisted Instruction

In teacher-assisted instruction, the teacher guides brainstorming and discussion among the whole class; interaction is student–student and teacher–student. Think-pair-share is an example, with pairs of students quickly sharing an idea based on the teacher's question, and the teacher then facilitating whole group sharing and discussion.

In this mode, the teacher does not lecture and give answers. When a student asks a question, other students respond rather than the teacher. Small groups or the whole class agree that an answer is correct, appropriate, or applicable based on supporting evidence and reasoning. Teacher-assisted instruction empowers and guides students to think and talk as scientist apprentices. Through thoughtful questioning techniques, the teacher facilitates and probes to encourage critical thinking, responds to student questions with meaningful questions that engage them in further dialogue with each other and with the teacher, and promotes the revision or review of their interpretations based on the evidence at hand. As students construct meaning from their explorations and text, the teacher may deem it necessary to intervene — by providing further evidence, raw data, or other resources or interactions — so as to model closer examination of evidence to correct misconceptions. The teacher should be aware that some students may need to interpret information that appears to contradict deeply held beliefs learned at home or in their communities. By providing a safe environment in which to express ideas, the teacher allows students to accommodate interpretations or test new ideas, while continuing to build understanding based on empirical and quantitative evidence.

APPLICATIONS FOR ENGLISH LEARNERS

The teacher ensures that English learners can participate in a variety of ways. First, the teacher frequently combines visuals, such as word walls, with "teacher talk," emphasizing key words and concepts. English learners can glance at word walls to "pull" words they want to incorporate when answering questions or participating in class discussions. Second, the teacher uses controlled speech, tailoring the wording of some questions for novice English learners and some for intermediate and more advanced English learners. Differentiated questioning gives all students the opportunity to participate in class discussions.

When an English learner student responds (and the answer is acceptable), the teacher may use "scientific rephrasing" to clarify the idea for all students and model desired academic discourse. The rephrasing is most helpful to the English learner if it is at a level just above what the student produced independently. The student might repeat the teacher's "rephrased statement" but should not be overtly asked to do so. For all students, scientific rephrasing helps them gradually develop much more sophisticated academic discourse. This can happen in a safe, respectful environment. Additionally, English learners have greater opportunity to comprehend concepts and thought processes when much of the class discussion involves redundancy among students. For instance, students may be invited to indicate agreement by restating the teacher's or another student's statement.

In teacher-assisted instruction, before individual students are asked to reply, the teacher may use think-pair-share, giving students a minute to think, then a minute or so to share answers with a partner before beginning a whole class discussion. This allows English learners to say their ideas comfortably with a partner before "going public" in front of the class. Think-pair-share is another way to build in redundancy, allowing English learners to hear an important concept described in slightly different ways, first in pairs and then in a whole class discussion.

Peer-Assisted Instruction

In peer-assisted instruction, small groups of students interact and learn as a team through collaborative or cooperative activities. Before students begin complex group activities, the teacher may need to model the expected group learning behaviors and establish rules of conduct. Students teach each other and learn together while the teacher monitors, guides, and models as necessary.

APPLICATIONS FOR ENGLISH LEARNERS

Some basic steps prepare students to work effectively in teams or small groups and ensure that English learners will be able to participate and learn. The teacher who designs effective cooperative and collaborative activities makes sure that an activity is cognitively challenging for everyone while varying the language demands that are necessary to participate and contribute. The activity itself will be structured in such a way that necessitates collaboration and discussion.

By making sure the group work directions and expectations are clear, the teacher also clears the way for a focus on learning. In classrooms with English learners, directions should be written as well as oral. For the teacher, writing the directions before giving them orally is also an opportunity to check that they are clear.

Sometimes student groups misbehave or become passive because they do not understand the concepts or the task instructions, so the teacher may need to initiate group work by modeling expected behaviors and gradually shift ownership of the group learning process to the students. Assigning roles is one way to help groups manage their interactions and structure successful participation for everyone. For example, a novice English learner in a group could participate as the illustrator of key concepts while more English proficient students are assigned to act as facilitator, writer, or reporter. With more experience and success, students can choose their own roles or collaborate more interdependently.

The grouping decisions a teacher makes should be strategic, sometimes grouping English learners by primary language, sometimes including them in groups with no other English learners, sometimes grouping students by other characteristics, and sometimes allowing students to choose groups by topic or interest. In a classroom where a strong community has been established, students might sometimes be allowed to choose groups by friendship, so long as everyone understands that no students must feel unwanted. (Figure 1.4 is one teacher's description of the grouping decisions she makes in a classroom where most students are English learners.)

FIGURE 1.4. **One Teacher's Grouping Decisions**

Following is a brief scenario of a high school science classroom where the teacher shifts among teacher-directed, teacher-assisted, and peer-assisted instruction.[9] This scenario shows the advantages of grouping students by their primary language. Other grouping criteria should be used as well (e.g., social characteristics, topic choice, science literacy).

Classroom setting. I speak only English and I have 35 students in my class, most of whom are English learners, spanning five languages (Spanish, Vietnamese, Mandarin, Tagalog, and Russian). There are eight lab stations in the room.

Grouping. Often I plan flexible student groupings for lab activities, mixing students by primary language, English literacy, and/or science literacy. Other times I allow students to select their own groups, and they usually select friends who speak their language. Today, I allow students to self-select, and most do so by their primary language. One station has Mandarin speakers, another Vietnamese, another Tagalog, two have Spanish speakers, and one station has native English speakers. My single Russian speaker sits with the English speakers.

Modeling. For this lesson, I start by conducting an experiment in front of the class. As we summarize each step of the experiment, I fill in key words on a graphic organizer on the board. (Soon in the year I will shift and just give procedural directions, students will initiate group experiments, and we will conclude with a class discussion in English that incorporates visuals such as graphic organizers.)

Group learning. Then students conduct the same experiment at their lab stations. They discuss in whichever language they choose, take notes about what they observe, and make illustrations. I have given English learners prepared notes with sentence frames (three levels of support corresponding to three levels of English proficiency). I walk around to answer questions and ensure that they are all learning successfully. Later, when I model the English responses to the questions, all students — even the most recently immigrated English learners — must write in English. Discussions within the self-selected groups of English learners are typically a mix of English and primary language, depending on the group members' needs and comfort levels. Later, when we have the full class discussion in English, the most limited English proficient learners will have a good idea of what is being said because it was first discussed within the homogeneous language group. For example, a new student will have spoken only Vietnamese while more proficient English learners discussed concepts in English with a little Vietnamese thrown in. If the new student didn't seem to understand, another Vietnamese speaker would have explained in Vietnamese.

The advantage to having students use their language of choice for peer-assisted learning and problem solving is that the focus stays on the science content. Students are not inhibited by their variable ability to communicate in English, so I feel more comfortable that they can really understand the concepts in the day's experiment.

Discussing. Next, I lead a whole class discussion in English about what they observed. I use the same structured format every time: (1) What did you do? (2) What did you observe happening? and (3) Why did it happen? I write students' answers as English sentences on an overhead transparency projected so that they all can see. Students copy the sentences in their notebooks in English and make connections to their lab notes. I find that repetition of common questions helps orient my English learners and provides a familiar context.

My newest student, who is at the beginning English learner level, benefits from listening to good oral models about content that is both familiar and meaningful, although I do not expect him to fully comprehend all that other students are saying. I assist other English learners to communicate their ideas by providing vocabulary, cues, and other structures that help them convey their thinking. The more proficient the English learner, the more elaborate I expect his or her comments to be. I do not ask "dumbed-down" questions, but I do adjust questions to be comprehensible for my English learners. When they finish responding, I selectively rephrase answers to model science discourse and incorporate key vocabulary. This scientific rephrasing benefits all students in the class.

DIFFERENTIATING INSTRUCTION

Differentiating instruction[10] means using a variety of instructional strategies that target the diversity of students in the classroom — students with different learning styles, interests, special needs, and those who are also English learners. For English learners, differentiation means tailoring a specific strategy to fit their language levels. It does not mean creating an individualized lesson for each student. It means planning a variety of ways for students to learn new concepts and read new material. It also means controlling speech and using word walls, visuals, and small group learning activities to make input more comprehensible for English learners.

For example, a science teacher who has English learners at two or three language levels (rather than all five) may use the same teaching strategies for all students but differentiate by offering two or three levels of support with a given strategy. In the case of note taking, all students are taught to take notes, and the teacher gives English learners templates with two or three different levels of text already completed, according to their language level. The most novice English learners receive a template that only requires filling in key words and phrases, with pictures for support. Templates for English learners at a higher level present sentence starters and transition words between sentences to help students write connected ideas.

Many of the strategies that help English learners comprehend science texts can also help everyone in the class. Leading students to access their prior knowledge and introducing key vocabulary are standard ways to engage all students in what they are about to read. As an advance organizer that benefits all students, the teacher can also introduce the text's key features and illustrations. In the explain stage, the teacher can read the textbook with the class and "think aloud" about key concepts in the process. Students should also have alternative texts available in a range of readability levels. (Textbook and trade book publishers often produce core science content at various reading levels.) Texts that are brief and interspersed with pictures or illustrations help English learners comprehend while reading. Websites are invaluable for providing alternative texts focused on a given concept or topic, and they often have a high ratio of pictures and graphics to text as well as hyperlinks to key words and related topics.

Other ways the teacher differentiates for English learners include accompanying oral presentations with visuals to help students listen with greater comprehension, giving English learners note-taking outlines or sentence starters to help them capture key concepts in a textbook that they struggle to read, and providing hands-on activities to help English learners "see" and actively engage in learning science concepts and procedures. Presenting the big picture or main idea as a glimpse of what to anticipate prepares English learners to concentrate on what is most important, and then delivering carefully scripted chunks of information allows them time to process it. Connecting instruction to students' experiences and offering choices heighten all students' interest and personalize instruction at a motivational level.

Some students learn better as members of small groups, and small group talk gives English learners a chance for language repetition and practice, so differentiation also means planning for collaborative and cooperative learning activities. The message of differentiation is to be aware of all the ways students are different and to plan ways to teach that capitalize on those differences. Figure 1.5 summarizes a number of ideas in this chapter that apply to differentiating instruction for English learners.

FIGURE 1.5. Lowering the Language Barrier for English Learners

The following classroom techniques have been found effective in lowering the language barrier and differentiating instruction for English learners:

>> Tap into prior knowledge to give students richer context for what they will learn. At the same time, activating prior knowledge lets students anticipate vocabulary and terms they are likely to hear and enables them to use context to guess words they do not know.

>> Provide wait time after asking a question — it may take English learners extra time to process back and forth in their primary language and English as well as to understand the question itself.

>> Have students discuss with a partner or in small groups relevant information from prior science lessons or personal experience; monitor group discussions, and then use a few examples to share with the class. Use flexible grouping in terms of primary languages spoken, English proficiency, general science knowledge, friendships, and other criteria.

>> Use multimodal presentations — visuals, word walls, hands-on experiments, etc. — during direct instruction and when summarizing or reviewing.

>> Repeat and rephrase important concepts, keeping periods of lecture or reading brief and concise but highly contextualized. Present new words in the context of the lesson and apply words during the lesson, pausing to emphasize each key word.

>> Use tiered lessons that address the same standards and topics but that adjust the difficulty level to challenge without frustrating students. For example, plan opportunities to restate a chunk of oral instruction in simpler form for English learners, perhaps while other students do seatwork; provide texts at different reading levels; assign seatwork tasks that differ in language demands; assign learning activities to small groups in which more proficient English speakers rephrase concepts and English learners are assigned less language-demanding parts of the task.

During assessment, the teacher also differentiates. For example, if students are to write about what they have learned, they are not uniformly presented with a blank sheet of paper and the general direction to "Explain the cycle of rock formation." Some English learners will more appropriately be asked to respond orally to a series of guiding questions. Others may be provided with sentence starters or graphic organizers that help them communicate what they have learned. Often, graphic organizers and other strategies implemented during instruction are also appropriate for helping English learners communicate during assessment. Figure 1.6 presents an example of assessment differentiation that accommodates English learners at different levels of proficiency.

FIGURE 1.6. Assessment That Accommodates Different Levels of English Proficiency

In the example below, the teacher provides assessment accommodations at three levels of English proficiency. The goal is to learn as much as possible about what English learner students have or have not understood about science content, not to demonstrate that they are not yet proficient in English.

>> Beginning English learners are given a template and asked to visually represent key ideas in pictures, diagrams, or graphic organizers. Students include labels and complete simple sentence starters as appropriate to their level of language development (Igneous rock looks _____. Igneous rock is formed when _____.).

>> Intermediate level English learners complete a visual representation and also complete sentence frames that help them connect ideas (Igneous rock looks _____; sedimentary rock looks _____. The difference is a result of their formation: igneous rock is formed by _____; in contrast, sedimentary rock is formed by _____.).

>> More advanced English learners use a graphic organizer to help write a composition that follows a model (introductory statement, description of each key point with supporting evidence, and summary, conclusion, inference, or generalization) with or without paragraph starters.

In later chapters, the ideas explored in this chapter about the 5 Es model, modes of instruction, and differentiation will be expanded and elaborated upon with specific tools and scaffolding techniques. In the next two chapters, however, we pause to consider the implications of language acquisition theory for classroom practice, and we explore students' language abilities at five levels of English proficiency.

ENDNOTES FOR CHAPTER 1

[1] Bybee, R.W. (1997). *Achieving scientific literacy: From purposes to practices*. Portsmouth, NH: Heinemann.

[2] National Research Council. (1999). *How people learn: Bridging research and practice*. Washington, DC: National Academies Press. See also NRC's *How students learn: History, mathematics, and science in the classroom* (2005).

[3] Weiss, R.P. (July, 2000). Brain-based learning: The wave of the brain. *Training & Development*, 20–24. Retrieved February 6, 2006, from http://www.dushkin.com/text-data/articles/32638/body.pdf.

[4] Krueger, A., & Sutton, J. (Eds.). (2001). *Edthoughts: What we know about science teaching and learning* (p. 2). Aurora, CO: Mid-continent Research for Education and Learning.

[5] The definitions of the 5 Es are adapted from *Strategic Science Teaching* (2002), a framework developed by the California Curriculum and Instruction Steering Committee Science Subcommittee and California Department of Education.

[6] Vang, C. (2004). Teaching science to English learners, *Language Magazine*, 4(4). Adapted with permission of *Language Magazine*, http://www.languagemagazine.com.

[7] Wormeli, R. (2005). *Summarization in any subject* (p. 5). Alexandria, VA: Association for Supervision and Curriculum Development.

[8] Black, P., & William, D. (1998). Inside the black box: Raising standards through classroom assessment. *Phi Delta Kappan*, 80(2), 139–149. Retrieved February 6, 2006, from http://www.pdkintl.org/kappan/kbla9810.htm.

[9] McCall-Perez, Z. (2005). *Grouping English learners for science*. Unpublished manuscript. Adapted with permission.

[10] A number of sources inform this discussion of differentiating instruction. For example:

Cole, R.W. (Ed.). (1995). *Educating everybody's children: Diverse teaching strategies for diverse learners;* and (2001). *More strategies for educating everybody's children*. Alexandria, VA: Association for Supervision and Curriculum Development.

Gregory, G., & Chapman, C. (2001). *Differentiated instructional strategies: One size doesn't fit all*. Thousand Oaks, CA: Corwin Press.

Silver, H.F., Strong, R.W., & Perini, M.J. (2000). *So each may learn*. Alexandria, VA: Association for Supervision and Curriculum Development.

Tomlinson, C.A. (1999). *The differentiated classroom*. Alexandria, VA: Association for Supervision and Curriculum Development.

Tomlinson, C.A., & McTighe, J. (2006). *Integrating and differentiating instruction: Understanding by design*. Alexandria, VA: Association for Supervision and Curriculum Development.

CHAPTER 2

Understanding Language Development

Language is central to teaching and learning every subject. Teachers use language to help students learn content; students use language to explore content and to express what they have learned. Normally, children acquire a first language at home from their caregivers. By the time they reach school age, they have a good command of the basic sentence structures and vocabulary of their first language. However, for children learning a second language, there is much more variation. Depending on home, school, and community circumstances, some children quickly learn a second language to a native-like degree, whereas others learn the second language much more slowly. This chapter will explore theories of first and second language acquisition, the differences between social, or everyday, language and academic language, and implications for classroom instruction. Terms that figure in or illuminate these discussions are defined in figure 2.1.

FIRST LANGUAGE ACQUISITION

Most people have no memory of learning a first language; those who have learned a second language, on the other hand, usually remember at least some key aspects of the experience. This raises the question of whether first and second language acquisition share basic similarities or whether they are very different.

There are three major first language acquisition theories: behaviorist; innatist; and interactionist.[2] Since first language acquisition largely takes place during the first few years of life, these theories have no implications for teaching in upper-grade classrooms; however, we will see later that these core concepts show up again in theories of second language acquisition.

Behaviorist Theory

Behaviorists believe that children learn by receiving positive or negative reinforcement for their behaviors; these rewards and punishments then shape their future habits. For language acquisition, this would mean that children listen to spoken language in their environment and try to imitate the language they hear. When they produce correct forms, they would be praised, and when they produce incorrect forms, they would be corrected or misunderstood, resulting in the reinforcement of correct (or adult-like) use of language. Three predictions about language acquisition can be made based on behaviorist theory: (1) Children imitate what they hear. (2) Adults correct children to reinforce "correct" (adult) forms of language. (3) Children respond to the corrections by producing the correct forms. Each prediction can be tested by looking at the reality of first language acquisition.

Children imitate what they hear. This is true to a certain extent. Children do imitate quite a bit at certain stages of language acquisition, usually around age two to three years. However, young children rarely repeat exactly what they hear. They usually leave out function words and repeat only content words. For example, a child hearing an adult say, "I'm going to the store now," might repeat this sentence as, "Going store now." It is unclear how children would learn the full set of sentence structures from getting reinforcement on these abbreviated sentences.

FIGURE 2.1. **Linguistic Terms**

Language. The word "language" in English describes two different concepts. The first is the abstract capacity humans have to represent thoughts, opinions, desires, and so forth in an external system that can be communicated to others (such as by sounds or signing). The second is the concrete, specific language used by a group of people, such as English, Spanish, Chinese, and American Sign Language. Another division is between direct and secondary representations of language. Speech and sign languages of the deaf (as developed by deaf people in a deaf cultural environment) represent the vocabulary and structures of language systems directly. Writing, as well as sign systems developed to represent a spoken language (such as signed English), are secondary since they represent spoken words and structures in another form.

Typically, young children learn direct language systems without formal instruction, by interacting with others in their environment, whereas they need specific instruction to learn secondary systems such as reading and writing. However, second language learners may need to learn both oral and written representations of their new language at the same time and may not be able to fully develop second language speech before starting to learn writing. Therefore, second language learners may also need explicit instruction in learning spoken language to accelerate their development.

Dialect. A dialect is a regional, social, or cultural variety of a wider language. Everyone speaks a dialect since everyone belongs to a particular regional, social, and cultural group at any given time. (In fact, each person has his or her own individual way of speaking — an idiolect.) The predominant dialect in a society is the one that becomes standardized in dictionaries and pedagogical grammar books, and this is called the "standard language." For example, standard English is the variety of English used by educated, middle-class speakers.

The standard language is often the variety that is considered to have "correct" grammar, while differences in the grammars of nonstandard varieties are considered "incorrect." However, this is simply a value judgment and does not reflect any underlying correctness in the system of that variety. Linguists have found that every language and every dialect spoken by human beings everywhere has a complete and rule-governed system.[1] Thus, from a linguistic point of view, there are no "primitive," "inadequate," or "bad" languages or dialects.

Grammar. In linguistic terms, grammar is the system of rules for word formation, sentence structure, and pronunciation in a given language. Linguists develop descriptive grammars to describe the systematic rules underlying the languages or dialects they are studying. In schools, teachers tend to focus on prescriptive grammar rules — those that describe the structures of language that are considered proper or correct according to society, usually corresponding to the rules of the standard language in that society. Second language English learners will, of course, be taught standard English in school. However, teachers should be aware that students will also pick up elements of other varieties of English as they socialize with their peers.

Adults correct the form of children's language. This is true when children are older and already have a command of basic sentence structure. However, most often, especially with young children, adults respond to the content of the child's speech, rather than to the structure. Adults often respond as if they understand the child's approximations of language. For example, when a child points to an animal and says, "That cow," an adult might respond, "Yes, that's a cow," giving the child positive reinforcement for using an incorrect sentence structure, or, "No, that's a sheep," but not, "No, you must say, 'That is a cow.'"

Children respond to corrections by using correct forms. As children progress in their language learning, they typically go through a stage when they overgeneralize grammatical patterns and use structures adults never use, such as "I goed," or "two foots." While they are in this stage, no amount of adult correction or modeling has any effect. The children continue using these incorrect (but more regular) forms until the stage passes and they start using the irregular forms such as "went" and "feet." Thus, it appears children are figuring out these structures through some internal process and not from adult feedback.

Behaviorist theory can explain how children learn basic vocabulary and routine phrases (such as "bye-bye" or "thank you") but not how they learn complex sentence structure.

Innatist Theory

Proponents of the innatist theory reject the behaviorist explanation for language learning and posit that, instead of being learned as a behavior, language seems to be acquired similarly to other innate skills, such as walking. All children are born with the capacity to acquire the skill of walking and, as they develop, they go through stages — crawling, standing, walking with support — that eventually lead to walking upright. Adults don't have to teach children how to walk by explaining the mechanism of walking or how to put one foot after the other — we assume children will learn to walk on their own, as long as their environment does not restrict or discourage them. Similarly, innatists believe children are born with the capacity to acquire language — they do not need to be taught language; instead, children innately go through stages that lead to speaking like an adult. Adults simply need to provide an environment in which children can figure out the rules of language on their own. Some of the central evidence for first language acquisition as an innate biological ability is summarized below.

Children experience uniform stages and attainment. All normally developing children go through similar stages of language acquisition at similar times, ultimately acquiring the basic vocabulary and sentence structures of the language(s) spoken with them. This is true across cultures, even when the environments are very different, including different ways caretakers interact with and speak to children.

First language must be acquired during a critical developmental period. Children in unusual circumstances who are not exposed to language before puberty do not appear able to learn adult-like language later in life. People learning a second language before puberty may be able to attain native ability to use a language, whereas people who learn a second language after puberty rarely attain native-level ability. As with some other biological functions, such as vision in humans, it appears that a first language must be acquired within a certain developmental period or it will be acquired only incompletely, if at all.

Children master the system of their first language without explicit evidence of all its possibilities. Children eventually learn the full system of their first language or dialect, even though they may not hear examples of all the specific language structures they eventually know and even though they are not instructed in or corrected about all the structures. In natural speaking, adults do not always use complete, well-flowing sentences. (A look at an unedited transcript of natural speech will show this.) They typically speak with fragments, false starts, unnoticed mistakes, repetitions, unsignaled corrections of noticed mistakes, etc. Children hear this natural speech without receiving explicit information about which parts are the incomplete, repeated, or uncorrected structures, and which are complete and correct. Thus, they must be starting out with some underlying knowledge about what language is and what the possible structures of human language are.

Innatist theory can be used to explain why a first language is learned without being taught. The details of the actual processes children go through and what underlying knowledge must be present in the mind for this to happen are still being studied.

Interactionist Theory

If exposure to adult language is all children need to learn their first language, then the question arises whether children need other people around to learn from or whether they could simply pick up their first language from TV or radio. There is strong evidence that children do not necessarily pick up a full system of language solely from passive exposure; it may be possible to learn some vocabulary and phrases in that way, but it appears that children learn how to produce complex forms by actually interacting with other speakers. The interactionist theory is based on this observation.

Proponents of the interactionist theory also point out that when adults or older children speak with younger children, they often automatically adjust their language, speaking more slowly and clearly, using simpler vocabulary and structures, and often repeating or paraphrasing. They may also respond to a young child's simple utterance with a grammatically complete adult version or an expansion. For example, if a child says, "Doggie sleeping," an adult might say, "Yes, the doggie is sleeping," or "The doggie is sleeping on the rug." While it is not clear that any particular interactive strategies are required to ensure a child learns language, the interactionist theory is built on the idea that some type of interactive communication is necessary for children to develop the full range of complex structures in a language.

Interactionist theory points to the environmental factors that must be present for children to learn language. When parties in a language interaction show what they do and do not understand, children are able to "test" and practice the system they are learning and try new or different ways to communicate.

SECOND LANGUAGE ACQUISITION

In the right circumstances, young children are able to successfully learn a second language without explicit instruction. On the other hand, adults typically need explicit instruction and much guided practice; even then, they often cannot attain native-like ability in a second language. Adolescents fall somewhere in between; while they may be able to pick up social language more quickly than adults, they may still need explicit instruction to become fully proficient in the grammar and academic language of their second language. The theories described below were originally developed in response to adults' incomplete second language acquisition. With the expansion of multilingual populations in schools, these theories have been applied to children's and adolescents' second language learning in the classroom as well. Some of these theories are directly related to the first language acquisition theories described previously.

Behaviorist Theory

As noted, behaviorists believe that language learning takes places through repetition and reinforcement. Behaviorist theories of second language acquisition predict that second language learners will make mistakes in their second language based on the already learned patterns in their first language. The main teaching method based on these theories, the audiolingual method, involves repetition drills, with a focus on getting learners to use correct pronunciation and grammar from the beginning. While this method results in adults being able to produce a series of learned phrases for a specific context, it does not give learners a basis from which to communicate freely in other contexts.

APPLICATIONS FOR ENGLISH LEARNERS

Repetition and pattern drills can be very useful for teaching set phrases or new vocabulary, and they are also useful for helping shy students use oral language, since with choral repetition, chants, or songs they can speak along with a group instead of being singled out. However, for learning more complex structures and communicative abilities, other methods need to be used.

Creative Constructionist Theory

This theory is based on the application of the innatist theory of first language acquisition to second language acquisition. Its best known proponent is Stephen Krashen, who developed a theory of second language learning consisting of five hypotheses.

First of all, the **acquisition-learning hypothesis** proposes that learning a second language is different from acquiring one. Learning involves conscious study of the forms of language, usually in a formal classroom environment, whereas acquisition of a second language would be similar to what happens during first language acquisition — learners pick up language by hearing and using it, without any explicit instruction.

According to the **monitor hypothesis,** acquired language produces fluent usage and intuitive judgments about the correctness of language forms, whereas with learned language, a "monitor" must apply specific learned rules to speech or writing to make sure it is correct.

The **natural order hypothesis** states that rules of a language are acquired in a certain order, with some predictably acquired earlier and others later. This natural order is not affected by teaching. This hypothesis recalls the stages of first language acquisition.

In order to acquire language, learners must receive "comprehensible input." The **input hypothesis** states that comprehensible input is the combination of structures that the learner already knows, plus enough new structures so that the learner can still comprehend; this is written as the formula $i + 1$. The input hypothesis holds that when the learner is exposed to new language in this way, it can then be acquired.

Finally, a learner's affective state can affect which input is acquired or not. The **affective filter hypothesis** states that when the "affective filter" is up — that is, when the learner feels anxious, self-conscious, or unmotivated — less acquisition will occur. When the filter is down and the learner feels relaxed and motivated, more acquisition will occur.

APPLICATIONS FOR ENGLISH LEARNERS

While Krashen's hypotheses are difficult to test and have not been proven empirically, they have intuitive appeal and have helped to move second language teaching away from grammar-book learning and toward more authentic, interactive methods.

The concept of comprehensible input has clear implications for the classroom, for native speakers and English speakers alike; while teachers should provide oral and written input to students near their proficiency level so they can comprehend the meaning, teachers should also provide some language, in context, just above students' proficiency level to help them acquire new language.

In addition, we know affective factors affect all types of learning; a fearful mind is closed to learning, while a relaxed mind is open to learning. As noted in the previous chapter, teachers who provide a respectful, caring classroom environment allow students to feel relaxed and to more readily learn language and content.

Interactionist Theory

As with first language acquisition, interactionists believe that people learn a second language by interacting with native speakers in two-way conversations. In these language interactions, native speakers can be responsive to the needs of language learners by modifying their language with the explicit goal of making it comprehensible. Learners can negotiate their own comprehension by asking for clarification or repetition.

APPLICATIONS FOR ENGLISH LEARNERS

Second language learners will have more opportunities to learn language the more they get to interact with the teacher and classmates. Their language acquisition may be accelerated when the teacher provides rich, comprehensible input and encourages higher levels of production. There are a number of ways teachers can modify their language to support and anticipate the needs of their English learners:

Comprehension checks. The teacher checks to see if the learner has understood (e.g., "The beaker must be cleaned after use. What will you do with the beaker?").

Clarification requests. The teacher gets the learner to clarify something not understood (e.g., "Can you say that again?").

Repetition or paraphrase. The teacher repeats or restates an utterance (e.g., "Measure the height of the plant. Take a ruler and see how high the plant is, how many inches tall.").

Nonverbal cues. The teacher supports utterances with visual cues such as gestures, written words, or pictures.

Corrective feedback. The teacher judiciously rephrases the learner's speech with correct forms within the flow of interactive conversation.

LANGUAGE AT SCHOOL: SOCIAL LANGUAGE AND ACADEMIC LANGUAGE

As noted above, all normally developing children in an interactive environment acquire the basic structures of their first language by the time they start school. Many second language learners will also be able to pick up the basics of a second language in this way — interacting with peers and hearing their new language used around them at school and in the community. It is important to realize, however, that literacy (reading and writing) and specific content area skills, including the vocabulary and structures used, must be explicitly taught in order for students to learn them. For many second language learners, this means learning both a new everyday, or social, language and a new academic language at the same time. Because these two types of language are not learned in the same way, a student who is fluent in social language and can converse comfortably about people, places, and events is not necessarily fluent in academic language. Adolescent English learners with little or no prior schooling in their native countries may also be learning to read for the first time in any language.

Jim Cummins, a well-known researcher of bilingualism, calls social language "basic interpersonal communicative skills" (BICS), and the language of literacy and academics "cognitive/academic language proficiency" (CALP). A theoretical model Cummins developed for understanding the difference between BICS and CALP is described below. Full competency in BICS may take up to three years, and in CALP five to seven years.[3] Teachers should not assume that students must attain full fluency in BICS before advancing to content or learning activities involving CALP.[4] Students can develop both BICS and CALP at the same time, especially since the boundary between BICS and CALP is not absolute — vocabulary and structures overlap, and spoken academic language is not usually formal and polished, except for prepared speeches.

Contextual Support and Cognitive Load

Figure 2.2 shows how communicative activities vary along two axes — contextual support and cognitive load. Context-rich activities involve high levels of contextual support, such as voice intonation, gestures, etc.; context-reduced activities involve low levels of contextual support, as with telephone conversations or written notes or reports. The other axis is the degree of cognitive demand. Cognitively undemanding activities require less thought or simultaneous processing; cognitively demanding activities require more thought or simultaneous processing. Thus, students may be able to quickly master BICS, having the ability to effectively interact in their second language in quadrant A — in cognitively undemanding situations where there are many contextual supports, as in a conversation with peers on the playground. However, students may take much longer to master CALP, interacting effectively in their second language in quadrant D — in cognitively demanding situations with few contextual supports, such as when reading a textbook on their own or listening to a long academic lecture.

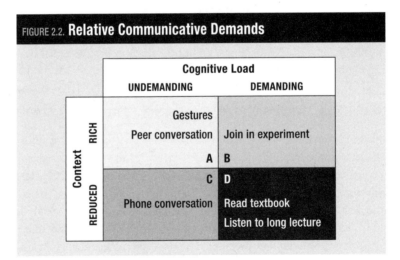

FIGURE 2.2. **Relative Communicative Demands**

APPLICATIONS FOR ENGLISH LEARNERS

Three major implications of the BICS/CALP theory apply to the instruction of English learners. The first is that teachers should not assume that students' fluency in everyday English is a sign of equal proficiency in using and understanding English for academic purposes. For example, a student may be able to converse easily with peers and with the teacher in one-on-one, face-to-face situations but may not as easily understand a lecture or a video presentation.

The second implication is that teachers can make academic content more accessible to English learners by providing more contextual cues during teaching and learning activities, such as connecting new lessons to students' prior knowledge, planning hands-on and interactive learning activities, and using pictures and graphic organizers. These contextual cues should be varied in order to tap into students' strengths in diverse learning modes such as auditory, visual, spatial, and kinesthetic.

The third implication is that teachers should carefully consider when to focus on language form correction versus when to focus on content material comprehension. When students are involved in cognitively undemanding activities, they will be able to turn their attention to self-correction or teacher correction of vocabulary choice and language forms. When they are involved in cognitively demanding activities, corrections will be a distraction and will impose an even higher cognitive load.

The suggestions in this chapter for working with English learners reflect the extra challenge for students learning a second language versus acquiring a first language, and they also take into account the increased cognitive load of learning academic language versus learning or acquiring social language. A summary of these suggestions appears in figure 2.3.

FIGURE 2.3. Teaching Tips That Reflect Language Acquisition Theory

» Use drills, choral repetition, chants, or songs for practicing new vocabulary and phrases. For example, a song or chant could be used to practice naming the elements, identifying the parts of the circulatory system, or labeling parts of the water cycle.

» When presenting information orally, repeat, rephrase, and expand on terms and structures.

» Check for comprehension by asking *wh–* questions ("What happens when…?") rather than yes-no questions ("Did you understand?").

» Show respect toward students and toward their first language and home culture. Build on their previous knowledge. Let students know they will not be ridiculed for making mistakes. Give them positive reasons to learn science and communicate in English.

» Make sure all students have opportunities to communicate both with one another and with the teacher. Vary the classroom organization among individual, pair, small group, and whole group work.

» Provide a variety of contextual clues when explaining new or abstract content. Connect ideas to students' previous experiences; involve them in hands-on activities; use pictures, graphics, and graphic organizers to support written and spoken information.

» Provide information and activities in different learning modes: auditory, visual, spatial, and kinesthetic.

» Choose carefully when to focus on correcting language forms. The best time for focusing on form is when students are involved in less cognitively demanding activities. Let them know in advance that form will be a focus. Focus on those forms that interfere with meaning, rather than minor details.

ENDNOTES FOR CHAPTER 2

[1] One exception is pidgins, which arise when people who speak different languages must communicate with each other yet do not have the time or desire to learn one another's language. The result is a simple word-based system without complex grammar. What is interesting is that in the next generation, speakers develop a more complex system from the pidgin, and this new variety is now a complete language in its own right.

[2] The sections of this chapter on first and second language acquisition are based on the overall conceptual organization of parts of Lightbown, P.M., & Spada, N. (1993). *How languages are learned*. Oxford: Oxford University Press.

[3] Hakuta, K., Goto Butler, Y., & Witt, D. (2000). How long does it take English learners to attain proficiency? *University of California Linguistic Minority Research Institute, Policy Report 2000–1*. Retrieved April 18, 2006, from http://faculty.ucmerced.edu/khakuta/research/publications.html.

[4] Marzano, R.J., & Pickering, D.J. (2005). *Building academic vocabulary teacher's manual*. Alexandria, VA: Association for Supervision and Curriculum Development.

CHAPTER 3

Understanding Five Levels of English Language Development

People do not learn either a first or second language all at once, but in stages — gradually increasing the use and comprehension of vocabulary and grammatical structures over time. This chapter addresses the stages, or levels, of second language acquisition, with a focus on academic language. In the upper elementary and secondary grades, the levels assume literacy in a first language, but this may not be the case for individual students, of course. Teachers will want a clear understanding of each English learner's previous academic experience and current English language development (ELD) level in order to best support content learning, appropriately assess what a student knows, and use that feedback to tailor instruction.

5 ELD Levels

Beginning

Early Intermediate

Intermediate

Early Advanced

Advanced

In this chapter, we provide information in a set of charts that teachers can use to quickly see what academic language skills can be expected at five ELD levels, judge their own English learners' current proficiency levels, and consider instructional strategies appropriate to each ELD level. In other words, the charts help teachers plan differentiated lessons for teaching and assessing students within their general levels of English language development.

The five levels — beginning, early intermediate, intermediate, early advanced, and advanced — represent distinctions often made in ELD standards. States differ in terminology; for instance, some states use the term ELP (for English language proficiency) and refer to performance indicators or benchmarks instead of standards. Title III of the federal No Child Left Behind Act refers to the five ELD/ELP levels and the labels used here.

Figure 3.1 shows five levels of English language development and very general student language behaviors at each level, along with teacher strategies appropriate to a given level. Figures 3.2 and 3.3 show more specific skills at each level, for grades 6–8 and grades 9–12, respectively.

For assessment purposes, the charts can be used as rubrics to judge the level of an English learner at any point in time. Often the only assessment data available to teachers are state test scores, which may be both too general and months too old to help guide instruction. The charts contain what we consider to be the essential academic language skills for instruction and assessment in any content area.

FIGURE 3.1. **Student and Teacher Behaviors at Five ELD Levels**

Level	Expected Student Performance	Teacher Strategies
Beginning	» Understand brief, very basic, highly contextualized input with visual support. » Respond to simple social talk and academic instruction by using gestures or a few words, phrases, and simple subject-verb-object sentences. » Read very brief text with simple sentence forms and mostly familiar vocabulary. » Exhibit many errors of convention (grammar, pronunciation, written mechanics).	» Use target vocabulary and sentence structure based on student's comprehension; repeat and rephrase; accompany oral instruction with visuals and hands-on activities. » Make connections to student's prior personal and academic experiences. » Ask basic, factual questions that can be answered with gestures or a few words. » Address various learning modalities. » Categorize learned words on wall charts, by concept, for easy reference. » Use brief texts with pictures at student's readability level. » Provide mostly completed chapter outlines with a few blanks for student to complete. » Scaffold writing (such as with models, sentence frames). » Assess student orally and perhaps use Cloze sentences and labeled graphic organizers.
Early Intermediate	» Understand brief, basic, contextualized input with visual supports. » Respond with increasing ease to a greater variety of social and academic communication tasks. » Respond by using phrases and simple sentences, more target vocabulary. » Read text with simple sentence structures and mostly familiar vocabulary. » Exhibit many errors of convention.	» Use vocabulary and sentence structure based on student's comprehension; repeat and rephrase; accompany oral instruction with visuals and hands-on activities. » Make connections to student's prior personal and academic experiences. » Ask fairly basic, factual questions that can be answered with a few words or simple phrases. » Address various learning modalities. » Categorize learned words on wall charts, by concept, for easy reference. » Use texts with pictures at student's readability level. » Provide partially completed chapter outlines with about 8–12 blanks for student to complete. » Scaffold writing (such as with models, sentence frames). » Assess student using graphic organizers and moderately supportive sentence frames.
Intermediate	» Understand and be understood in many basic social situations. » Understand more complex input, but still need contextual and visual support in academic language. » Respond by using expanded vocabulary and connected, expanded sentences. » Apply the English language skills that have been taught to meet immediate communication and learning needs. » Read text with mostly familiar vocabulary or participate in small group reading of texts. » Exhibit many errors of convention.	» Choose vocabulary and sentence structure based on student's comprehension; repeat and rephrase as needed; accompany oral instruction with visuals and hands-on activities. » Make connections to student's prior personal and academic experiences. » Ask critical thinking questions that can be answered with phrases and simple sentences. » Address various learning modalities. » Provide texts at student's readability level. » Teach student to use glossaries and his or her vocabulary notes as references. » Provide models and less scaffolding for writing. » Assess student using sentence frames/starters; follow with specific oral prompting for ambiguities.

FIGURE 3.1. **Student and Teacher Behaviors at Five ELD Levels (continued)**

Level	Expected Student Performance	Teacher Strategies
Early Advanced	>> Understand complex input appropriate for the grade level with some need for visual supports. >> Respond by using expanded vocabulary in expanded sentences. >> Combine the elements of the English language in complex, cognitively demanding social and academic situations. >> Read grade-level texts with preview of content and key words. >> Exhibit some minor errors of convention.	>> Use vocabulary and sentence structure normal for grade level. >> Make connections to student's prior learning. >> Ask critical thinking questions and encourage responses that are detailed sentences. >> Address various learning modalities. >> Provide texts at student's readability level and grade level. >> Provide models and minimal use of scaffolds for writing; integrate language arts and content-area activities and give feedback to continue developing language and writing skills. >> Assess student's independent writing; provide clear directions, writing models, and paragraph starters/outline.
Advanced	>> Fully understand input appropriate for the grade level. >> Respond with expanded vocabulary and connected, expanded sentences. >> Communicate effectively with various audiences on a range of familiar and new topics to meet social and academic demands; may need further linguistic enhancement and refinement to reach the level of native language peers. >> Read grade-level texts independently.	>> Use vocabulary and sentence structure normal for grade level. >> Make connections to student's prior learning. >> Ask critical thinking questions and encourage responses that are detailed sentences. >> Address various learning modalities. >> Provide texts at student's grade level. >> Writing may need minimal use of scaffolds; integrate language arts and content-area activities and give feedback to continue developing language and writing skills. >> Assess student's independent writing; provide clear directions.

FIGURE 3.2. **Academic Language Skills: Grades 6–8**

Skill	Beginning	Early Intermediate	Intermediate	Early Advanced	Advanced
Listen With Comprehension	Listen to and follow simple directions. Listen to teacher's simple questions, answers, and brief explanations aided by appropriate scaffolds. Show understanding by identifying one or a few key ideas using gestures and phrases.	Listen to and follow more complex directions. Listen to teacher's questions, answers, and brief explanations aided by appropriate scaffolds. Show understanding by identifying some key ideas using simple sentences.	Listen to and follow multistep directions. Listen to teacher's questions, answers, and explanations aided by appropriate scaffolds. Show understanding by describing key ideas using complete sentences with more details.	Listen to and follow multistep directions. Listen during teacher's lesson and engage in class discussion with visual aids. Show understanding by explaining key ideas using detailed sentences.	Same as early advanced.
Use Academic Vocabulary	Use basic social vocabulary and a few academic vocabulary words in simple phrases and sentences to communicate basic meaning in social and academic settings.	Use some academic vocabulary words in sentences to communicate meaning. Use context clues to understand a few unknown words.	Use expanded academic vocabulary in more detailed sentences to express ideas. Use glossary, knowledge of word parts, and context to understand some unknown words. Recognize multiple meanings of some words.	Use expanded academic vocabulary in detailed sentences to express complex ideas. Use knowledge of word parts and context as well as dictionary to understand unknown words. Recognize multiple meanings of many words.	Same as early advanced.
Ask and Answer Questions	Orally ask and answer simple factual comprehension questions about listening or reading passages using simple phrases and sentences.	Orally ask and answer factual comprehension questions about listening or reading passages using simple sentences.	Ask and answer factual and simple inferential comprehension questions about listening or reading passages using some detailed sentences.	Ask and answer factual and inferential comprehension questions about listening or reading passages using detailed sentences.	Same as early advanced.
Explain Main Ideas	Orally identify a main idea and a few details in a listening or reading passage using phrases and simple sentences.	Orally describe a main idea and some important details in a listening or reading passage using simple sentences.	Orally or in writing, explain the main ideas in a listening or reading passage by connecting to some important details.	Orally or in writing, explain the main ideas in a listening or reading passage by connecting to important details.	Orally or in writing, explain the main ideas in a listening or reading passage by connecting to important details and using expanded vocabulary.

FIGURE 3.2. **Academic Language Skills: Grades 6–8 (continued)**

Skill	Beginning	Early Intermediate	Intermediate	Early Advanced	Advanced
Use Writing Strategies	Organize and record information by displaying it in pictures, lists, charts, and tables.	Collect information from various sources, take basic notes, and write and revise a brief paragraph by following an outline.	Use strategies of basic note taking, outlining, and revising to structure drafts of simple essays or reports.	Use strategies of note taking, outlining, summarizing, and revising to structure drafts of mostly clear, coherent, and focused essays or reports.	Use strategies of note taking, outlining, summarizing, and revising to structure drafts of clear, coherent, and focused essays or reports.
Write Compositions	Create phrases and simple sentences. Write brief compositions that have a main idea. Exhibit many major errors of language conventions.	Write brief, simple compositions that include a main idea and some details. Exhibit many major errors of language conventions.	Write brief compositions that include a thesis and some supporting details. Exhibit few major and some minor errors of language conventions.	Write compositions that include a clear thesis and supporting details. Exhibit some minor errors of language conventions.	Write well-developed compositions that include a clear thesis and supporting details. Exhibit few, minor errors of language conventions.
Write Research Reports	Gather basic information as part of a group. Present information graphically with labels and write simple sentences. Exhibit many major errors of language conventions.	Gather more complex information as part of a group. Present information graphically and write brief summary paragraphs. Exhibit many major errors of language conventions.	Investigate a topic as part of a group. Develop a brief report that includes source citations. Exhibit few major and some minor errors of language conventions.	Investigate a topic and write a full report that conveys information; use technical terms, citations, and a bibliography. Exhibit some minor errors of language conventions.	Investigate and write reports that clarify and defend positions with evidence and logical reasoning; use technical terms, citations, and a bibliography. Exhibit few, minor errors of language conventions.
Communicate Critical Thinking	Compare and contrast. Identify cause and effect and sequential order relationships. Identify facts and opinions. Form basic hypotheses and conclusions.	Compare and contrast. Identify cause and effect and sequential order relationships. Distinguish between fact and opinion. Hypothesize and conclude.	Compare and contrast. Describe cause and effect and sequential order relationships. Distinguish between fact and opinion. Hypothesize, infer, generalize, and conclude.	Compare and contrast. Analyze cause and effect and sequential order relationships. Distinguish among fact, opinion, and supported inferences. Hypothesize, infer, generalize, and conclude.	Compare and contrast. Analyze cause and effect and sequential order relationships. Identify relative credibility of information. Hypothesize, infer, generalize, and conclude.

FIGURE 3.3. Academic Language Skills: Grades 9–12

Skill	Beginning	Early Intermediate	Intermediate	Early Advanced	Advanced
Listen With Comprehension	Listen to and follow simple directions. Listen to teacher's simple questions, answers, and brief explanations aided by appropriate scaffolds. Show understanding by identifying one or a few key ideas using gestures and phrases.	Listen to and follow more complex directions. Listen to teacher's questions, answers, and brief explanations aided by appropriate scaffolds. Show understanding by identifying some key ideas using simple sentences.	Listen to and follow multistep directions. Listen to teacher's questions, answers, and explanations aided by appropriate scaffolds. Show understanding by describing key ideas using complete sentences with more details.	Listen to and follow multistep directions. Listen during teacher's lesson and engage in class discussion with visual aids. Show understanding by explaining key ideas using detailed sentences.	Same as early advanced.
Use Academic Vocabulary	Use basic social vocabulary and a few academic vocabulary words in simple phrases and sentences to communicate basic meaning in social and academic settings.	Use some academic vocabulary words in sentences to communicate meaning. Use context clues to understand a few unknown words.	Use expanded academic vocabulary in more detailed sentences to express ideas. Use glossary, knowledge of word parts, and context to understand some unknown words. Recognize multiple meanings of some words.	Use expanded academic vocabulary in detailed sentences to express complex ideas. Use knowledge of word parts and context as well as dictionary to understand unknown words. Recognize multiple meanings of many words.	Same as early advanced.
Ask and Answer Questions	Orally ask and answer simple factual comprehension questions about listening or reading passages using simple phrases and sentences.	Orally ask and answer factual comprehension questions about listening or reading passages using simple sentences.	Ask and answer factual and simple inferential comprehension questions about listening or reading passages using some detailed sentences.	Ask and answer factual and inferential comprehension questions about listening or reading passages using detailed sentences.	Same as early advanced.
Analyze Main Ideas	Orally identify a main idea and a few details in a listening or reading passage using phrases and simple sentences.	Orally describe a main idea and some important details in a listening or reading passage using simple sentences.	Orally or in writing, explain the main ideas in a listening or reading passage by connecting to important details.	Orally or in writing, analyze the main ideas in a listening or reading passage by connecting to important details and using expanded vocabulary.	Same as early advanced.

FIGURE 3.3. **Academic Language Skills: Grades 9–12 (continued)**

Skill	Beginning	Early Intermediate	Intermediate	Early Advanced	Advanced
Use Writing Strategies	Organize and record information by displaying it in pictures, lists, charts, and tables.	Collect information from various sources, take basic notes, and write and revise a brief paragraph by following an outline.	Use strategies of basic note taking, outlining, and revising to structure drafts of simple essays or reports.	Use strategies of note taking, outlining, summarizing, and revising to structure drafts of mostly clear, coherent, and focused essays or reports.	Use strategies of note taking, outlining, summarizing, and revising to structure drafts of clear, coherent, and focused essays or reports.
Write Compositions	Create phrases and simple sentences. Write brief compositions that have a main idea. Exhibit many major errors of language conventions.	Write brief, simple compositions that include a main idea and some details. Exhibit many major errors of language conventions.	Write brief compositions that include a thesis and some points of support. Exhibit a few major and some minor errors of language conventions.	Write compositions that include a clear thesis and describe organized points of support. Exhibit some minor errors of language conventions.	Write compositions that provide evidence in support of a thesis and related claims and counterarguments. Exhibit few, minor errors of language conventions.
Write Research Reports	Gather basic information as part of a group. Present information graphically with labels and write simple sentences. Exhibit many major errors of language conventions.	Gather more complex information as part of a group. Present information graphically and write brief summary paragraphs. Exhibit many major errors of language conventions.	Investigate a topic as part of a group. Develop brief reports that include source citations. Exhibit few major and some minor errors of language conventions.	Investigate a topic and write full reports that convey information; use technical terms, citations, and a bibliography. Exhibit some minor errors of language conventions.	Investigate and write reports that clarify and defend positions with evidence and logical reasoning; use technical terms, citations, and a bibliography. Exhibit few, minor errors of language conventions.
Communicate Critical Thinking	Compare and contrast. Identify cause and effect and sequential order relationships. Identify facts and opinions. Form basic hypotheses and conclusions.	Compare and contrast. Identify cause and effect and sequential order relationships. Distinguish between fact and opinion. Hypothesize and conclude.	Compare and contrast. Analyze cause and effect and sequential order relationships. Distinguish among fact, opinion, and supported inferences. Hypothesize, infer, generalize, and conclude.	Same as intermediate.	Compare and contrast. Analyze cause and effect and sequential order relationships. Identify relative credibility of factual information. Hypothesize, infer, generalize, and conclude.

CHAPTER 4

Teaching the Language of Scientists

I n science, much of what students need to learn requires that they master specialized vocabulary and discipline-specific ways of using language, whether for listening, speaking, reading, or writing. Integrating language instruction into content instruction is a research-based approach that works, and effective science teachers do this for all their students.[1] For students who are also English learners, learning language in the context of learning science is not simply beneficial, it is crucial.[2] Language learning and content learning are inseparable — and reciprocal.[3] Integrating them accelerates English language development, shortens the delay before English learners have equitable access to content curriculum, and supports culturally and linguistically inclusive classrooms.[4]

This chapter describes the teacher's role in facilitating students' language use and presents some concrete steps for teaching new vocabulary. Finally, a number of tools are introduced that the science teacher can use to help students organize science concepts and vocabulary.

THE LEXICON AND DISCOURSE OF SCIENCE

Academic language that relates specifically to science is the **lexicon of science** — the set of terms scientists and science learners use to communicate about their subject matter. These content words and phrases have a specific meaning in the context of the discipline. For example, "biology," "Petri dish," "chemist," and "plate tectonics" all relate specifically to science and are clearly part of the lexicon of science.[5]

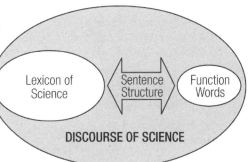

While some terms are exclusive to science, others overlap disciplines. For example, such biological terms as "conservative," "translation," and "replication" have different meanings in other disciplines. (Teachers in different disciplines who share a set of students may want to identify an interdisciplinary lexicon and coordinate vocabulary instruction so students easily see a word's meaning connections and discern any shades in meaning particular to a discipline.)

In addition, English learners may not be aware that fairly common words can be applied differently in different disciplines. For example, the function word "by" has many meanings depending on context, such as "by the river" in literature, "by 1803" in social science, "multiply 3 by 4" in mathematics, and "by osmosis" in science. Function words and phrases do not refer to anything in and of themselves. But they have important functions — to signal grammatical, logical, or rhetorical relationships. For example, "because," "for example," and "in order to" are common function words or phrases. (Figure 4.1 lists commonly used function words and phrases that English learners need to understand.)

To use the lexicon of science, English learners need to practice using it in sentences and extended discourse. Sentence structure governs the formation of sentences — the combination of content and function words into statements, questions, and commands.

At a level beyond the sentence, discourse involves use of language to convey extended expression of thought on a topic in connected speech or writing. A key aspect of the discourse of scientists is communication about the processes of science — for example, knowing how to provide an explanation supported by evidence, how to write a report of an experiment, and how to debate a current scientific issue. (Figure 4.2 lists important terms students need to understand for communicating about science processes related to investigations and experiments.)

FACILITATING STUDENTS' LANGUAGE USE

English learners at different developmental levels can all learn the lexicon and discourse of science. However, as we saw in chapters 2 and 3, the complexity of these language components will vary according to students' English proficiency. One way to think about this is that all students will learn the same science concepts, but the teacher will need to adjust the complexity of language he or she uses to explain these concepts depending on each student's English proficiency level.

In addition to adjusting and differentiating language for learners at different stages of English proficiency, the teacher also supports English learners (as well as "visual learners") with hands-on activities and visuals. Visuals might be real objects, pictures, illustrations, graphic organizers, word walls, board notes, or video clips.

The teacher repeats and rephrases for English learners, and provides adequate wait time (five to seven seconds) before asking for responses from English learners or students who need more time to process information. (As noted in chapter 1, wait time encourages deeper thinking and equalizes students' opportunities to respond.)

When providing corrective feedback to English learners, the science teacher focuses first on ideas and meaning, especially when the student is struggling to communicate complex concepts. In these cognitively demanding situations, the teacher might simply ignore grammar errors. Feedback in these instances takes the form of "scientific rephrasing" to help the student understand the science. For example, the English learner says, "I mix salt in water and it [looks at the word wall] dissolve." The teacher responds, "Yes, the salt dissolved in the water. The salt is the solute, and the water is the solvent." Notice that the teacher models correct verb usage but emphasizes the key academic words that had been taught.

During interactions that have a low cognitive demand, when the concept is simple or the answer is easy, the teacher can respond to incorrect grammar. Corrective feedback in such instances can be implicit by rephrasing a student's comment in a grammatically correct way. For example, the teacher asks students if they have read about a science topic in the newspaper lately. An English learner says, "Yesterday I see news

FIGURE 4.1. **Common Function Words**[6]

Function words and phrases are the necessary connectors for relating ideas and signaling their organization. Native English speakers learn them as a matter of course. For English learners, a special effort must be made to help them master these terms. Many of the words or phrases can be used as "sentences starters," while some connect ideas inside a sentence. They can be provided to English learners on posters to support oral language and in sentence frames to support written communication.

Giving a definition	is equal to	means	refers to	is synonymous with
	is the same as	in other words	consists of	in fact
Providing an example	for example	for instance	such as	is like
	including	to illustrate		
Adding more ideas	in addition	also	another	moreover
	furthermore	finally		
Sequencing	first…second	next	initially	before
	preceding	when	finally	after
	following	on (date)	not long after	now
	as	by (date)		
Comparing	same as	just like/as	in the same way	in comparison
	not only…but also	as well as	similarly	
Contrasting	different from	as opposed to	instead of	in contrast
	however	but	although	yet
	while	on the other hand		
Showing cause and effect relationships	because	as a result of	may be due to	since
	consequently	this led to	so that	nevertheless
	in order to	effects of	for this reason	if … then
	therefore	thus		
Describing problems and solutions	one answer is	one reason is	a solution is	the problem is
	the question is			
Expressing an opinion or conclusion	I think	I believe that	I predict that	I suggest that
	I conclude that	I deduce that	I speculate that	in my opinion
	I agree with ____ that			
Reporting findings or outcomes	I/We found that	I/We learned that	I/We discovered that	I/We observed (heard/felt/smelled) that
	____ told (explained/ mentioned to) me/us that	I now realize that	I want to find out more about	I am beginning to wonder about

FIGURE 4.2. **Common Science Discourse Patterns**

Originally compiled by Dobb[7] from the investigation and experimentation strand in the California science standards, this adapted list is a reminder of the many science activities and discourse patterns that students need to understand.

analyze	consult multiple sources	distinguish fact from opinion	illustrate	outline	replicate
anticipate	contrast	document	infer	persuade	report
calculate	defend a position	estimate	inquire	plan	request/provide assistance/ directions
cite discrepancies	demonstrate	experiment	interpret	predict	revise
cite information	describe	explain	investigate	propose	sequence
classify	design	explore	investigate cause/effect relationships	provide evidence/ rationale	solve
compare	determine	formulate	justify	question	state
conceptualize	disagree	hypothesize	make a claim	reflect upon	strategize
conclude	discuss	identify	measure	recognize	suggest
confirm	distinguish cause from effect	identify physical attributes	observe	record	summarize
construct charts/ graphs	distinguish constants from variables	identify properties/ relationships	organize	reformulate	support with facts

about a rocket hit a comet." The teacher's first move is to acknowledge a correct answer, and then to provide corrective feedback. "Okay," the teacher says, indicating that the student is on target. The teacher then immediately continues, "Yesterday you saw news about a rocket that hit a comet." The student replies, "Yes, I saw it." As English learners often do, the student here recognizes and acknowledges the corrective feedback by using the corrected word or phrase.

Feedback like this, whether in the form of scientific rephrasing or corrective feedback, is a natural and unthreatening aspect of learning in classrooms where a safe climate has been established. Students understand that the teacher will not embarrass them and their classmates will not ridicule them.

Simple routines for encouraging student participation in class or small group discussions can also ease the anxiety English learners may feel about sharing their ideas. Think-pair-share, for partner sharing prior to class sharing, was discussed in chapter 1. Another routine, heads together, facilitates small group discussion (see figure 4.3). For whole class discussions, a ball-toss routine can get even reluctant high school students to speak (see figure 4.3). Luck-of-the-draw is another option for reducing students' resistance to speaking (see figure 4.3).

FIGURE 4.3. **Encouraging Student Discussion**

Heads Together. Heads together is similar to a huddle in football. The classroom is arranged in small groups, with each group seated around a work table or with their chairs pulled into a circle. The teacher gives students a discussion question with a brief time limit. In each group, students stand and lean their heads close together to quietly discuss and reach agreement. When everyone in a group sits back down, the teacher knows the group is finished. Heads together minimizes classroom noise, helps to engage all students, and signals the start and finish of small group discussions.

Toss-the-Ball. Toss-the-ball gets all students to participate during whole class discussions. The teacher tosses a ball to a student who then responds (some teachers allow the first student to say "pass"). After answering, the student tosses the ball to a classmate. This student can use sentence frames (or not) to agree, disagree, build on the first student's response, or offer a different idea. The ball can continue traveling around the room for as long as seems productive. A variation is to have different questions or vocabulary words written on tape secured to different areas of the ball. The student who catches the ball answers the topmost question.

Luck-of-the-Draw. Systems to randomize turns can relieve students of the need to volunteer to speak, making it possible for shy or reluctant students to "succumb" to the dictates of fortune. For example, in class discussions, the teacher might have all students' names written on slips of paper or tongue depressors and collected in a cup. The last student to answer draws the name of the next person to respond. Likewise, in small groups, speaking turns might depend on rolling dice or picking a card. It is often the case that students appreciate the chance to speak — they just don't want to volunteer.

Finally, the science teacher should expect English learners as well as native English speakers to vary the formality of their use of academic language depending on the context. Written academic language is typically the most formal. Formal oral presentations would also be held to the highest standards for language use. However, most spoken academic language is not formal. It falls between the formality of written academic language and the informality of social language. Even university lectures and learned discussions tend to be fragmented, containing insertions, repetitions, and deletions.[8] Similarly, the academic speech of English learners will be informal and should not be corrected for every misstep. By being strategic about when to address errors, the teacher increases the effectiveness of the feedback that is offered.

TEACHING VOCABULARY

Science textbooks and many science books and online articles highlight key vocabulary words that are critical for understanding the topic[9] and that many students typically will not know. But English learners may not know many additional words in the text that will be crucial for their full understanding of the topic. Teachers who have observed and noted the language proficiency and backgrounds of their students will be able to strategically select and teach the key words all their students, including their English learners, need to know.

To support English learners, the science teacher will be very deliberate about what vocabulary to teach, and when. Vocabulary words should be taught within the context of learning scientific concepts, not in isolation.[10] The science teacher can plan to introduce new words as part of the engage, explore or explain stages in the 5 Es model and repeatedly apply these new words when students speak, read, and write. For example, new vocabulary can be introduced and applied in the engage stage, while connecting to prior knowledge (students' experiences or previous lessons); in the explore stage during an experiment or investigation; or in the explain stage while completing a reading assignment.

Six Steps for Teaching Vocabulary

As noted, not all new vocabulary is taught at the same time. Following are six steps for teaching key vocabulary words that a teacher can use when planning a science lesson. The teacher chooses the key words in the textbook that students, particularly English learners, are unlikely to know; identifies which words are most important; targets when to teach the words (during which of the 5 Es); and ensures ample time to teach these words. Most key words will be science terms; some words may be function words or adjectives or adverbs that enrich the meaning of a science term.

STEP 1. IDENTIFY WORDS ALL STUDENTS NEED TO KNOW

Determine which of the key words for a day's lesson is best taught at each of three stages (the words may be those highlighted in the text or those identified by the teacher[11]):

>> **Engage stage words.** At this stage, common definitions and examples from students' prior knowledge are addressed. Later, during content instruction, these words are revisited and refined with scientific definitions. (For example, reference to "waves" during the engage stage may only elicit students' basic knowledge of ocean waves; during instruction, the scientific definition and characteristics of wave types would be added.)

>> **Explore stage words.** These words are taught during content instruction, such as when students are conducting an experiment, or listening to a brief lecture.

>> **Explain stage words.** These words are also taught during content instruction, such as when students are reading the textbook.

STEP 2. IDENTIFY WORDS ENGLISH LEARNERS NEED TO KNOW

The science teacher searches for other words in the lesson that English learners likely do not know. English learners must be able to comprehend these key words when reading the textbook, listening to teacher talk, and engaging in class discussions. The words may include the following:

>> scientific terms, such as "observe" and "oscillate";

>> support words, such as "ripple" and "disturbance"; and

>> function words or phrases, such as "as a result of."

The teacher stars or highlights the highest-priority words — those which

>> are absolutely essential to understanding the lesson;

>> should not be substituted for with more common words; and

>> are the key words used in many science lessons, what Susana Dutro and Carol Moran[12] call the "brick and mortar words" — science concepts and the general vocabulary that supports or connects the concepts. (For example, we can break down into brick and mortar the following sentence: "The cell divides as a result of its volume being too large for the cell's DNA to control its metabolic activities optimally." The words "cell," "volume," and "DNA" are examples of bricks. The phrases "as a result of" and "too large for" are examples of mortar.)

Additional unknown yet important words often crop up during a lesson. However, teaching unknown words without a lesson plan for them is rarely as effective as when they have been anticipated. The more the teacher knows his or her students, the better. Fewer surprises are then likely and more effective instruction is possible.

For words that will not be addressed in the lesson plan, the teacher plans comfortable, risk-free ways for students to flag words they do not know during the lesson. For example, students might use any of the following strategies:

>> Circle unknown words in text handouts.

>> Use dry highlighter tape or sticky notes to identify unknown words in the textbook.

>> Write unknown words in a section of a note-taking template that the teacher monitors, helping particular students or groups with quick definitions (when there is time, students can use dictionaries and glossaries for unknown words).

>> Use dialogue journals to let the teacher know what concepts and words they do not understand.

STEP 4. CHOOSE KEY WORDS FOR A DAY'S LESSON

The teacher sets a limit on how many new words to present in a day's lesson. When the number of new words is overwhelming, the teacher can shelter the language load (e.g., by using resource materials with more controlled language and illustrations or by scanning text and substituting synonyms that students already know).

While teaching only up to 10 words is typically desirable, if the lesson can still be understood, more than 10 words might be allowable when some are synonyms/antonyms or closely related in a word family. Also, English learners who know a concept in their native language and only need the translated English word(s) may be able to handle more new words. Some of these known words may be cognates[13] — words that have the same meaning and the same or similar spellings since they derive from the same ancestor language — or words one language has borrowed from the other. The teacher's judgment about how many words to introduce is based on knowing the students and what words they know or likely know, how difficult the new words are, and the need to maintain the focus of instruction on science content.

It may be that some words that don't make the cut are synonyms of higher-priority words and can be linked to them. Other lower-priority words might be defined in context or simply replaced with known words, to make a sentence comprehensible and allow understanding of the concept to build.

STEP 5. BUILD FROM INFORMAL TO FORMAL UNDERSTANDING

The science teacher needs to consider whether to introduce new words before or after covering a science concept, keeping in mind that learning new words naturally progresses from informal to formal understanding.[14] Informally, the teacher starts with students' own definitions, explanations, examples, or drawings. Activating students' prior experiences or knowledge cues the teacher into ways to help guide students' thinking. Their responses may be incomplete or very general at first; the teacher can gradually add multiple meanings or specificity. The teacher also teaches students how to use context clues to determine the meaning of a word. Students keep glossaries and look up definitions in dictionaries later, in the more formal process of building understanding.[15]

For example, the word "frequency" may be at first interpreted in terms of more familiar contexts, as in a bus stops frequently — very often — to pick up passengers along its route. Other students may have heard it being used in the news, at sporting events, in literature, or in prior science courses. Students who have musical backgrounds may also relate it to tuning instruments. The science teacher extends their understanding as they study the electromagnetic spectrum, learn about sound (pitch variation), or learn about light and wave dispersion. Once students learn the essential meaning applied to all of these interpretations, they may refer to "frequency" as a recurrence or repeated event within a particular length of time, having the essential understanding to apply it as they go on to learn and explore different contexts in which the word "frequency" is used.

STEP 6. PLAN MANY OPPORTUNITIES TO APPLY KEY WORDS

Students need many opportunities in class discussions and writing to hear, repeat, and apply key terms to deepen and sustain their understanding of them. The science teacher consciously reuses the key words, emphasizing them during teacher talk by pausing and saying the word slightly louder or pointing to the word on a wall chart.

In addition to word charts and word walls, students should have key terms readily available in notebooks or personal glossaries in which they continually enter new words, brief definitions, and other cognitive supports such as illustrations or diagrams. The personal glossary primarily serves each student as a ready reference, but the teacher can draw quick reviews from student glossaries and solicit white-board answers, for example, of words, definitions, or meaningful sentences based on recent entries.

Students can also work in groups to manipulate and understand new vocabulary. For example, small groups can select graphic organizers and use them to sort lists, either class-brainstormed or teacher-supplied. Organizing factors can vary — by hierarchy, compare-contrast, cause-effect, and so forth.

The science teacher structures numerous ways for students to practice using new vocabulary in meaningful situations and stretches English learners to produce new word forms (e.g., "a hypothesis" from "to hypothesize"). Marzano and Pickering offer a range of activities and academically oriented games for reviewing and applying word meanings.[16]

TOOLS FOR UNDERSTANDING VOCABULARY AND CONCEPTS

Teachers have many options for teaching vocabulary and helping students organize and understand concepts. Figure 4.4 presents a synthesis of tips gleaned from a number experts for teaching academic vocabulary effectively.

To help teachers put these tips to work, seven tools are particularly useful. It is likely that the teacher would use three or four of these in combination to support students in a given lesson. Any combination of tools would almost surely include word walls or glossaries. The concept organizer is another key tool, best used daily for perhaps two or three crucial words. Sentence frames and vocabulary self-ratings can be useful as pre- and post-assessments. The word form chart can be inserted at any point during a lesson, and the features matrix is useful both during a lesson and for review. List-group-label is another way for students to review, allowing them to consolidate conceptual as well as vocabulary knowledge.

We recommend that science teachers use these tools in support of hands-on inquiry and experiments, not only when lecturing or having students read an assignment. Each is described in detail on pages 46–52.

FIGURE 4.4. Tips for Teaching Vocabulary Words[17]

» **Routinize instructional steps.** When introducing new words, follow a set routine so that students can focus on the vocabulary and not be concerned with the teaching steps. For example, students might consistently expect to see the word, hear the word, say the word, and write and define the word along with a showing sentence while the teacher writes the word on the word wall or a word chart.

» **Use supportive visuals.** Incorporate visuals such as real objects, pictures, movie clips, illustrations, and graphic organizers to "show" the word as it is presented orally. Plan meaningful ways to show words as you say and define the words within the context of the lesson.

» **Teach word parts.** Show English learners common elements among certain words by teaching word parts (roots, prefixes, suffixes) and how to use word parts. Roots, prefixes, and suffixes are important for defining and connecting many science terms. If possible, teach the native language cognates to build dual language proficiency.

» **Apply key words repeatedly.** Create opportunities for students to practice using new words in a variety of structured and unstructured situations. Plan opportunities to apply the set of new words within the real context of academic conversations and writing.

» **Observe and assess.** Observe students' use of key words orally and in writing during the lesson. For summative assessment, select a few words from the list of new words for quick quizzes. Use periodic review assessments to test a random sampling of words.

WORD WALL, GLOSSARY

Purpose	Students have important vocabulary words readily available to use when they talk and write about their ideas. Word walls and glossaries help English learners use academic language.
Description	Word walls or word charts list important academic words and phrases, organized by topic. These lists are posted around the classroom so that students can easily see and use them.
	Glossaries are personal collections of important words that students define in English and/or with an illustration; they may also translate the words into their native languages. In addition to those words that students choose for themselves, the teacher may request that all students make specific entries.
Use	Word walls and word charts are not just for primary grades — high school students will use more academic vocabulary in their talking and writing when they have a rich bank of words easily available.[18]
	The teacher adds words to wall charts as new words are introduced. In addition to key science terms, the teacher may include other words — function words and modifiers — that are important for English learners. Students can refer to the charts and apply the words in speaking and writing. Words might be organized alphabetically or by word families, within topic areas. Word lists can be maintained on a computer for updating and for alternative organizations. Parallel to the class lists, students might build personal glossaries as a quick reference — especially for writing tasks — including cognates and synonyms in their native languages.
	There is a range of what teachers can do with a wall chart, from simply listing the words on chart paper with a brief visual cue (stick-drawings) to having a preformatted wall chart to identify word use and add definitions (mirroring what students have in their notebooks). Word walls can be written on a transparency form and projected as the teacher is introducing concepts or students are working on an exploration; in this way, it becomes an ongoing tool to model spelling, use, definitions, etc. The complexity of the format depends on the grade level, the number of English learners in the class, and the emphasis needed for content knowledge transfer.
	In a final variation, large file cards can be tacked to a corkboard with the words on one side and definitions and illustrations on the other side. This allows for categorizing ideas and manipulating relationships as well as for quick review or assessment.
Examples	›› A student glances at the word wall (see-observe, saw–observed) and says, "I *observed* that . . ."
	›› Lists of function words include examples of their use (e.g., "Tide pool ecosystems are *different from* kelp forest ecosystems." *(not the same as)*
	›› Key content words (nouns, verbs, adjectives) are paired with synonyms and antonyms.
	›› Lists of words are categorized by similar characteristics with category labels, such as below:

Structure and Function of the Digestive System			
Organ Structure (part of speech)	Organ Function	Related Illness	Illustration
mouth (n.)		cancer from smoking	
teeth (n.)	to cut, tear, grind food	cavities from not brushing	
salivary glands (n.)	to make swallowing food easier		
–saliva (n.)	uses enzyme amylase to break starch molecules into sugar molecules		starch 0000 + saliva (amylase) = sugars 00

SENTENCE FRAMES

Purpose   English learners have a "starting place" for saying and writing their ideas, as well as models of correct grammar usage and paragraph construction.

Description   Students are prompted to create sentences based on frames that provide some sentence parts and leave blanks for others. In some cases, pictures scaffold students' understanding and ability to complete the blank portions of the sentences.

Use   Frames help English learners produce a complete sentence or paragraph to communicate knowledge. In addition, sentence frames can be used to model English grammar, while paragraph frames can be used to model writing skills. Most of a sentence is provided for English learners at early stages (beginning, early intermediate), and sentence starters are provided for more advanced English learners (intermediate, early advanced). Sample sentence frames are displayed on the wall for quick reference.

Examples
» A bank of sentence starters is posted in the classroom. The teacher directs students to relevant frames and encourages students to use them during a discussion or writing activity.

» After the class reads about oceans, for example, the teacher presents a relevant sentence frame on the board and models its use. Then the teacher directs students to use the sentence frame as an idea starter during a planned small group or whole class discussion in response to prepared questions.

» After a class field trip to a local aquarium, for example, the teacher writes questions on the board and gives students sentence frames for responding orally or in writing, working on one question at a time. In the following example, a beginning English learner is working to complete field notes that are provided as sentence frames. The teacher uses oral questions to prompt the student and provide context for the sentence frames.

Teacher: Which tide pool animal is your favorite? Why?

My favorite tide pool animal is the_____

because it _____.

Teacher: How does it protect itself?

It has _____ that it uses to protect itself.

Teacher: What does it eat?

It eats _____. This is its prey.

Teacher: What likes to eat it?

_____ likes to eat it. This is its predator.

VOCABULARY SELF-RATING

Purpose   Students rate their knowledge of key vocabulary words before the lesson, after the vocabulary instruction part of the lesson, and after the content part of the lesson. This activity alerts students to the key words they will learn and helps them plan and monitor their learning. It helps students be aware of what they know and take responsibility for what they need to learn. The teacher adjusts lessons based on a quick review of students' personal rating sheets.

Description   A student's self-rating is personal; it may be shared with the teacher, but it is not graded. Students rate whether they know the word (+), do not know the word (–), or are not sure (?) at three different points: before the lesson begins, after specific vocabulary instruction, and after instruction on science content (at the end of the entire lesson).

Use   » Step 1: The teacher pronounces each word and students rate their knowledge level. This alerts students to words they need to learn. A quick survey of completed columns alerts the teacher to which words to emphasize.

   » Step 2: Students rate the words again after vocabulary instruction. Students see their growth and the teacher sees which words need more attention during the content lesson.

   » Step 3: Students rate the words once again and see their growth, while the teacher sees which words need reteaching and what content related to the words may not be sufficiently understood.

Example

Vocabulary Self-Rating			
Name: _____			
Lesson Topic: _____ Period: _____			
+ I am sure I know it – I am sure I don't know it ? I'm not sure			
Word (form)	Before Lesson	After Vocabulary Instruction	After Content Instruction
organ (n.)			
amylase (n.)			
enzyme (n.)			
absorb (v.)			
diffuse (v.)			

CONCEPT ORGANIZER

Purpose	English learners investigate in depth the meaning or multiple meanings of selected academic vocabulary.
Description	One concept organizer is used for each new word. This tool organizes a variety of ways to understand a word's meaning: sentences, synonyms, definitions, characteristics, examples, and non-examples. If present, a prefix is noted as a clue to a word's meaning. Characteristics are phrases that may give slightly different aspects of the word's meaning. The definition broadly covers the characteristics.
Use	The teacher gives the word in context, perhaps in a sentence from the textbook or other science resource book. The class brainstorms synonyms, definitions, characteristics, examples, and non-examples. Each student culminates the concept organizer by writing his or her own showing sentence. Use the following sequence of steps to teach each new word:

>> Point to the word on the word list and pronounce it; ask students to repeat the word.

>> With class participation, define and describe the word, using at least a synonym or definition, and a showing sentence or brief explanation:

— Identify one or several synonyms that students already know.

— List characteristics.

— List examples and non-examples.

— Create a student-friendly definition or adapted definition from the textbook or a dictionary, or brainstorm a definition with students; write it on the board or a transparency while students write it on their organizers.

— Create a showing sentence that implicitly defines and applies the word or create a brief explanation (a phrase up to a few sentences).

>> Show a visual representation (picture, illustration, movie clip, or graphic organizer) especially for classifier words (e.g., mammal); students may make illustrations on their concept organizers.

Students' concept organizers can be written on 5×7 index cards, hole-punched in the top left corner, and organized on a large key ring.

Example

invertebrate, n. (or adj.)	
Prefix & Meaning: in– not or without	Root: vertebra
Synonym: spineless	
Characteristics: – no vertebrate bones or spinal column; might have a shell – animal — insect or marine animal	
Definition: (general meaning or for a specific context) animal having no spinal column	
Examples: snail, worm, ant, butterfly, sponge, clam, shrimp, jellyfish	Non-Examples: lizard, fish
Showing Sentence: Invertebrates are animals that have no backbones.	
Illustration: ⟵ worm	

WORD FORM CHART

Purpose	English learners see the different forms of a key word and can refer to them when writing.
Description	A word is changed into basic grammatical forms such as noun, verb, adjective, and adverb. Multiple meanings may be addressed, or not. Plural spellings may be included when they depart from the –s or –es form.
Use	This tool may supplement the concept organizer. Word forms may be given to students in the science period, or they may brainstorm or look up answers during their language arts period. This may be a homework assignment or small group activity.

Example

Verb	Noun	Adjective	Adverb
observe	observation observer observatory	observable	
hypothesize	hypothesis hypotheses	hypothetical	hypothetically

LIST-GROUP-LABEL

Purpose	Groups of vocabulary words are taught as word families, or new words are added into existing family groups after they are taught. Organizing words into word families and concept categories promotes schema formation and conceptual understanding. For reference and review, students can quickly search the charts and recognize relationships.
Description	Known words relevant to a lesson are organized by categories given by the teacher or created by student groups. The teacher guides students to see how words are associated. Word families can be classified by synonym/antonym or conceptual characteristics (e.g., mammals, states of matter, types of volcanoes).
Use	The whole class may brainstorm an initial list of words about a topic and the teacher records them on the board or a transparency; then small groups organize them by categories and give labels to the categories. When words have multiple meanings in different disciplines, teachers of different subjects can collaborate and teach the multiple meanings explicitly, so students see both the connections and subtle differences in meanings.
Examples	The teacher asks student groups to construct a chart associating types of waves with their characteristics. Students then share group charts and construct a class chart to ensure common knowledge.

List-Group-Label	
Waves	
Types	Characteristics
mechanical transverse longitudinal	gas, liquid, solid crests, troughs compressions, refractions

List-Group-Label	
Soils	
Types	Characteristics
clay	fine-grained, usually yellow, stiff, and less than 0.04 mm grains
sand	granular, loose, multicolor, rough, and larger than 0.06 mm grains
loam	mixed sand, silt, and clay with humus (e.g., dead leaves)

FEATURES MATRIX

Purpose Students see concept words and their relationships visually reinforced. Similar but frequently confused terms are clarified; similarities and differences within a category are graphically represented.

Description Characteristics are compared across a range of objects or topics. Cells in the matrix are marked + (present) or − (not present).

Use Students work in pairs or small groups to complete a matrix first modeled by the teacher. The matrix may be completed as part of note taking during reading and instruction or to summarize and review afterward. Student groups may be encouraged to add characteristics in a few additional columns on the right. After completing the matrix, students use sentences orally or in writing to describe the characteristics present or not present in an object or topic. (For example, "A lizard has a spinal column, legs, and scaly skin, but it does not have mammary glands or an outer shell.")

Example

Features Matrix					
+ yes		− no		? not sure	
Animal	Spinal Column	Mammary Glands	Outer Shell	Scaly Skin	Legs
snail	−	−	+	−	−
lizard	+	−	−	+	+
snake	?	−	−	+	−

Features Matrix					
+ yes		− no		? not sure	
Mechanical Model of Fluids Transport	Dump Model	Squirt Model	Siphon Model	Vacuum Model	Other: _____ ___
has ability to move "stuff"	+	−	+	+	
has continuous flow	−	−	+	?	
circulates (back to start)	−	−	−	−	

ENDNOTES FOR CHAPTER 4

[1] Harlev, R. (2005). Contented learning. *Language, 4*(9), 22–27.

[2] Short, D. (1993). Assessing integrating language and content. *TESOL Quarterly, 27*(4), 627–656.

[3] Clegg, J. (Ed.) (1996). *Mainstreaming ESL: Case studies in integrating ESL students into the mainstream curriculum.* Clevedon, UK: Multilingual Matters.

[4] Gibbons, P. (2002). *Scaffolding language, scaffolding learning.* Portsmouth, NH: Heinemann.

[5] Some states list key science terms included in state content standards.

[6] Adapted with permission from English Learners and the Language Arts (ELLA), San Francisco: WestEd, 2003.

[7] Dobb, F. (2004). *Essential elements of effective science instruction for English learners* (2nd ed.) (p. 66). Los Angeles: California Science Project.

[8] Swales, J.M. (2005). Academically speaking. *Language Magazine, 4*(8), 30–34. Conclusions based on analysis of 1.7 million transcribed words of University of Michigan speeches from lectures, office hours, meetings, dissertation defenses, and so forth collected between 1997 and 2002.

[9] Marzano, R.J., & Pickering, D.J. (2005). *Building academic vocabulary teacher's manual.* Alexandria, VA: Association for Supervision and Curriculum Development. The authors have identified nearly 8,000 words in national standards documents in 11 subject areas for grade spans K–2, 3–5, 6–8, and 9–12.

[10] Maatta, D., Dobb, F., & Ostlund, K. (2006). *Strategies for teaching science to English learners* (p. 44). In Fathman, A.K., & Crowther, D.T. (Eds.) *Science for English language learners: K-12 classroom strategies.* Arlington, VA: NSTA Press.

[11] The two websites below for identifying (and defining) key terms are representative of the online vocabulary resources available for teachers and students:

The American Heritage Student Science Dictionary lists 400 important science words and definitions: http://www.houghtonmifflinbooks.com/booksellers/press_release/studentscience

Oxford University Press has a list of the 250 most common science words: http://www.oup.com/elt/catalogue/teachersites/oald7/oxford_3000/science?cc=gb

[12] Dutro, S., & Moran, C. (2003). Rethinking English language instruction: An architectural approach. In G.G. Garcia (Ed.), *English learners: Reaching the highest level of English literacy.* Newark, DE: International Reading Association.

[13] English and Spanish have many cognates from Latin-based words (e.g., animal/animal, problem/problema, capacity/capacidad, current/corriente, dictionary/diccionario, nuclear/nuclear, and system/sistema). False cognates, or falso amigos, on the other hand, can trip students up (see http://allinfo-about.com/spanish/vocabulary/vo-falsoamigos.html for the tricky actual/actual, discutir/discuss, ignorar/ignore, realizar/realize, and others).

[14] Marzano, R.J., & Pickering, D.J. (2005). *Building academic vocabulary teacher's manual* (p. 16). Alexandria, VA: Association for Supervision and Curriculum Development.

[15] Print dictionaries recommended by Kate Kinsella for use with English learners include the following:

Early intermediate level in grades 4–9: *The Basic Newbury House Dictionary of American English* (1998) by Heinle & Heinle.

Intermediate level in grades 6–12: *Newbury House Dictionary with Thesaurus* (2004) by Heinle & Heinle; *Longman Dictionary of American English* (1997) by Longman.

Advanced level in grades 7–12 and college: *Longman Advanced American Dictionary* (2000) by Longman.

Beginning through advanced levels: *Thorndike Barnhart Dictionary* (1999) by Scott Forsman.

[16] Marzano, R.J., & Pickering, D.J. (2005). *Building academic vocabulary teacher's manual.* Alexandria, VA: Association for Supervision and Curriculum Development.

[17] Baker, S.K., Simmons, D.C., & Kameenui, E.J. (1995). Vocabulary acquisition: Curricular and instructional implications for diverse learners. *Technical Report No. 14.* Eugene: University of Oregon, National Center to Improve the Tools of Educators. Kate Kinsella presents similar tips in her books and workshops about academic vocabulary development for English learners.

[18] Gibbons, P. (2002). *Scaffolding language, scaffolding learning.* Portsmouth, NH: Heinemann.

CHAPTER 5
Scaffolding Science Learning

In the field of learning, the elegant metaphor of "scaffolding" comes from the rough-and-tumble world of construction sites, where temporary frameworks of platforms erected around a building allow workers to reach with their drills, hammers, and brushes areas that otherwise would be out of range. Likewise, a science teacher uses scaffolding strategies to temporarily support students while they build new science skills and knowledge — at a higher level than they could reach without such assistance.[1]

Take note that scaffolding is not just another word for helping. As Pauline Gibbons specifies, "It is a special kind of help that assists learners to move toward new skills, concepts, or levels of understanding. Scaffolding is thus a temporary assistance by which a teacher helps a learner know how to do something, so that the learner will later be able to complete a similar task alone."[2] Gibbons warns that scaffolding is not about simplifying a learning task and ultimately watering down curriculum. The importance of scaffolding is that it allows a teacher to provide authentic and challenging tasks to all students, with the supports that allow them to be individually successful.

Almost all students need teachers who guide and support them as they construct new knowledge. English learners (among other students) require extra support if they are to master a rigorous, standards-based curriculum. Every student has the right to equal access to the curriculum. Scaffolding is a way for teachers to keep content at a high level yet still accessible to the variety of students in the classroom.

We begin the chapter by discussing how to use scaffolding strategies, including four "big ideas" to simplify their use and an outline of a lesson plan that integrates vocabulary strategies from chapter 4 and scaffolding strategies described in this chapter. Next, we present four options for scaffolding science reading materials. Last, we describe seven specific strategies that allow science teachers to scaffold learning for English learners. These strategies were chosen because they apply to teaching science, can be learned fairly quickly, and can be practiced in the classroom fairly easily. Rigorous research has found these strategies to be effective with the general student population.[3] In the absence of similar research about methods that close the achievement gap for English learners,[4] we propose, and other experts on teaching English learners concur, that these strategies should also be effective for English learners when adapted to address their English language challenges.

We assume that many science teachers are familiar with at least some of these strategies; what may be new is how they can be integrated, possibly increasing their effectiveness for English learners. In addition, we imagine that some teachers may know how to use a strategy in a whole class lesson but not know how to differentiate, or modify, its use to fit different levels of English learners.

If a strategy is entirely new for a teacher, it might be necessary to go to other resource materials or experienced colleagues to learn more about using it effectively. However, we purposefully selected strategies that are fairly quick and easy to learn; and we excluded some powerful strategies such as cooperative learning because of their complexity and the time they take to learn to use proficiently.

HOW TO USE SCAFFOLDING STRATEGIES

The scaffolding strategies in this chapter benefit all students in the classroom and can be implemented in whole class activities – but differentiated according to students' needs. The teacher structures the use of a strategy to give appropriate kinds of support to students at different English language development levels to ensure that all students can access rigorous content.

Because scaffolding, in teaching as in construction, is temporary, the teacher has a plan to reduce or fade the level of support provided as students become increasingly accomplished. The teacher's goal is to move learners from dependence on teacher-designated strategies to independent application of strategies for their own purposes and in a variety of settings. So, when introducing a new strategy, the teacher models its use and discusses its purpose. The teacher discusses classroom rules that underpin using the strategy, such as respecting others' opinions, valuing diversity of beliefs, and other acceptable social learning behaviors. Then the teacher guides student practice. Finally, when students have sufficiently internalized the strategy and understand its purpose, process, and optional uses, they apply it independently during group and individual learning tasks.

We use the example of graphic organizers to concretely show the shift from teacher to student for the selection and use of this specific scaffolding technique:

>> The teacher shows a model of a graphic organizer such as a web or bubble organizer, explains its purpose, and shows how to use it with a very specific example.

>> The teacher provides small groups with a graphic organizer template that is blank or partially completed to different degrees depending on a group's ELD level; groups complete the task together while the teacher monitors and checks for understanding; then they debrief.

>> Students work in groups to apply the graphic organizer in a few lessons and then work independently to apply it. When working independently, some students will have almost complete, some partially complete, and some blank organizers according to their need for scaffolded support.

>> As students collect a bank of graphic organizers (e.g., webs, Venn diagrams, T-charts, cycles), the teacher guides students to compare and contrast their application in different contexts or for different tasks, so students learn how to select the appropriate organizer for new topics or tasks.

>> When the teacher systematically and frequently has students use the organizers, students build fluency and self-reliance.

The chart below describes four "big ideas" that teachers should keep in mind as they group students and select strategies to differentiate instruction according to students' needs.

BIG IDEAS THAT SIMPLIFY DIFFERENTIATING INSTRUCTION	
Big Idea 1: Group Students to Provide Access for All Proficiency Levels	A teacher might need to tailor a strategy for only two or three levels of English learners. Many teachers do not have students at all five English learner levels in their classrooms (see chapter 3 for details about the five levels); for those who do, one approach is to combine students at contiguous proficiency levels into three groups. First, form an English fluent group by combining early advanced and advanced English learners, along with native English speaking students, who can all benefit from the same types of scaffolding strategies. Second, form an English intermediate group by combining early intermediate students who are ready for more challenge with intermediate English learners. Third, form an English novice group by combining early intermediate English learners who still need extensive linguistic support with beginning learners.
	The teacher assigns students to work together in these novice, intermediate, and fluent groups during the occasional activities that benefit learners interacting in a homogenous group. Most of the time the teacher forms groups of students at different English proficiency levels so that students have multiple opportunities to practice a variety of communication skills, including rephrasing, asking for clarification, and using their native language. An advantage of heterogeneous grouping is that novice English learners experience "model" language use by more advanced English speakers. The teacher still must provide differentiation for English learners within these groups, such as note-taking templates that scaffold writing for novice, intermediate, and advanced English learners.
Big Idea 2: Use Strategies That Work for All Students	Some instructional strategies work well for all or most students and do not need differentiation for English learner levels. English learners as well as other students whose strength is learning visually benefit when visual representations (e.g., video clips, pictures, graphic organizers) accompany oral discussions of new concepts. English learners and other students whose strength is learning kinesthetically benefit from hands-on lab experiments and investigations. Teachers who know their students' backgrounds can explain difficult, abstract science concepts by offering analogies that are relevant to students' lives and cultures.
Big Idea 3: Use A Strategy Throughout the Lesson	A specific strategy need not be limited to one time use within one of the 5 Es or for one learning activity. A strategy can be used throughout much of a unit of study. For example, the teacher may introduce a word wall and graphic organizer as simple charts during the engage stage, add and expand words and concepts during explain and elaborate stages, and guide the students to apply their developing vocabulary during discussion, reading, and writing activities. Routine use of a strategy throughout the year helps all students focus on learning science concepts rather than on learning how to use new strategies.
Big Idea 4: Make Connections Between Strategies	The teacher can identify connections among strategies and make those connections explicit for students. For example, a concept organizer zooms into the most important words on a word wall, providing more depth of understanding. In addition, one strategy can be embedded in another. For example, sentence frames and visuals such as pictures and brief graphic organizers can be embedded in Cornell-style notes.

* Adapted from collaborative work between WestEd and Secondary Science Education in Los Angeles Unified School District, May 2007.

The following chart on pages 58 and 59 graphically displays an outline for a lesson plan* of integrated strategies that flow through the 5 Es stages of a middle grade unit lesson about density and buoyancy. The strategies combine those from chapter 4 to teach vocabulary and strategies in this chapter to scaffold content learning. When a strategy does not need to be differentiated by English proficiency level, the cells in that section are left blank.

AN OUTLINE FOR A LESSON PLAN OF INTEGRATED STRATEGIES

Example		Conceptual Flow of Learning Activities within 5 Es			
		Overarching Question: What does density have to do with buoyancy?			
		Engage	Explore	Explain	Elaborate
		Floating Puzzles Mass & Floating	How Heavy?	Analyzing Data: Reading: What is Density?	
	Scaffolds for EL Learning	**Evaluate:** Formative (e.g., hand gestures, white boards, lab notes); Summative (e.g., quizzes, tests — oral prompting, complete graphic organizer and sentence frames according to English learner levels)			
	Reading and Media Materials	Video clip	Lab materials; notes template	Textbook chapter; leveled texts	
	Vocabulary: Enhanced Word Wall	Introduce words in advance organizer	Add words and informal definitions, pictures	Apply new words in discussions; formally define key words	Students apply vocabulary in writing
	Vocabulary: Concept Organizer		Students fill out concept organizer; put key words on ring cards	Students apply vocabulary in reading, writing	Students apply vocabulary; add more words to ring cards
	Sentence Frames		Provide template for lab notes; students refer to wall of key words and sentence starters during discussion and writing	Provide template for reading notes	
	Word Form List-Group-Label Features		Lab notes chart		
	Graphic Organizer	Circle Map	Add to Circle Map	Flow Map	Multiflow Map
	Think Aloud		Demonstrate lab activity	Model reading strategy	
	KWL Chart	K–W w/ visuals: elicit from students		L: elicit from students	L: elicit from students
	Think-Pair-Share		Table groups answer questions on lab demo		Table groups respond to questions about the elaboration
	Summarizing			Student triads take reading notes	

AN OUTLINE FOR A LESSON PLAN OF INTEGRATED STRATEGIES

Scaffolds for EL Learning	3 Classroom EL Levels		
	Novice	Intermediate	Fluent
	B/EI	EI/I	EA/A
	Heterogeneous groups for all activities except reading texts.		
Reading and Media Materials	Students read leveled text & take notes with teacher	Group of students read leveled text & take notes	Group of students read text & take notes
		Groups share information Revise notes	
Vocabulary: Enhanced Word Wall			
Vocabulary: Concept Organizer			
Sentence Frames	B/EI template: Identify key concepts	EI/I template: Describe key concepts	EA/A template: Explain, infer, generalize
Word Form List-Group-Label Features			
Graphic Organizer	Students identify key ideas	Students give examples, some details	Students give evidence, critical details
Think Aloud			
KWL Chart			
Think-Pair-Share			
Summarizing	Oral Retell	Oral summary	Note-taking template

HOW TO SCAFFOLD SCIENCE READING MATERIALS

English learners below the early advanced level may have difficulties independently reading a science textbook or other complete texts on science. To ensure that English learners can fully comprehend the content in science texts, teachers need to integrate strategies for scaffolding science reading materials into their lesson preparation and delivery. At a general level, we recommend assigning students to read sections in the textbook after the Engage and Explore stages, as well as providing supplemental or alternative text sources at different readability levels. More specifically, we recommend considering one of the four options below, each of which describes detailed steps for planning instruction using scaffolds with different types of reading materials.

Each option first identifies English learners' likely reading comprehension abilities at different proficiency levels, and then describes four steps for scaffolding reading materials, from selecting appropriate reading materials to guiding students in instructional activities that enhance their interaction with the text. Each option first identifies English learners' likely reading comprehension abilities at different proficiency levels, and then describes four steps for scaffolding reading materials, from selecting appropriate reading materials to guiding students in instructional activities that enhance their interaction with the text.

Option 1: Using Unaltered Textbook

English learners at the intermediate level and below will likely have difficulty independently reading and comprehending entire textbook units or chapters. Intermediate level English learners may be able to comprehend some shorter excerpts reading independently. The steps below will help all English learners access content in a science textbook.

Step 1. Identify excerpts in a conceptual unit of study that address the most critical or essential information that English learners need to understand.

Step 2. Provide engaging, concrete activities to front-load key content and functional vocabulary in context, building conceptual understanding during the Engage and Explore stages. Students can then reference word walls, concept organizers and graphic organizers throughout the lesson.

Step 3. Provide the excerpts identified in Step 1 along with advance organizers and meaningful questions for the students to answer. Use think alouds and model reading strategies such as reciprocal teaching and assisted note-taking, so that students will be able to apply metacognitive reading skills to make sense of text and record information in notebooks.

Step 4. Have students collaboratively read pre-selected textbook excerpts in small groups as part of the Explain or Elaboration stages, using graphic organizers and the modeled reading strategies. Two possible grouping options are: (1) students are grouped by shared native language so they can discuss cognates and concepts in their native language; (2) students are grouped by varying levels of English proficiency and literacy skills, so that students at higher levels can assist those at lower levels. Monitor groups to ensure all students are challenged and meaningfully engaged. Rotate among individuals or small groups, asking probing and clarifying questions.

Option 2: Using Annotated Textbook Excerpts

English learners at the beginning and early intermediate levels will likely have difficulty independently reading and comprehending annotated textbook excerpts. Intermediate level English learners may be able to comprehend annotated excerpts reading independently. The steps below will help all English learners access content in annotated excerpts from a science textbook.

Step 1. Identify excerpts in a conceptual unit that address the most critical or essential information that English learners need to understand. Annotate the excerpts by highlighting key words, defining or clarifying key concepts with notes in the margin, or adding illustrations. Make copies to hand out to the students.

Step 2. Provide engaging, concrete activities to front-load key content and functional vocabulary in context, building conceptual understanding during the Engage and Explore stages. Students can then reference word walls, concept organizers and graphic organizers throughout the lesson. Introduce the annotated excerpts during the Explore stage.

Step 3. Provide students with meaningful questions to answer, and use think alouds and model reading strategies such as reciprocal teaching and assisted note-taking, so that students will be able to apply metacognitive reading skills to make sense of the annotated text and record information in notebooks.

Step 4. English learners collaboratively read textbook excerpts in small groups as part of Elaboration stage. Monitor groups to ensure all students are challenged and meaningfully engaged. Rotate among individuals or small groups, asking probing and clarifying questions.

Option 3: Using Reading Materials at Various Readability Levels

English learners at the beginning level likely cannot independently read and comprehend brief texts at the lowest possible readability level, but can comprehend some ideas with assisted reading (e.g., being read to, in choral reading). English learners at early intermediate and above can independently read and comprehend texts at their readability level.

Step 1. Identify key ideas to find texts at students' readability levels, building resources from the librarian, ELD/English teachers, colleagues, classroom/city libraries, or district experts who provide resources for all teachers. Repeat the resource building process for key ideas in each conceptual unit.

Step 2. Front-load key academic vocabulary and build conceptual understanding during the Engage and Explore stages; build word walls, etc. Embed reading texts during the Explain stage or the Elaborate stage. Introduce contextualized and visually rich text resources during the Engage and Explore stages.

Step 3. Provide meaningful questions for the students to answer, and model note-taking using specific organizers, charts, tables or graphs, as most appropriate for the task.

Step 4. Each small group may be assigned the same or different text levels. Students read independently or in pairs (when paired students have the same text level) and then discuss and annotate concepts independently and/or as a group in a poster.

Option 4: Using Special Texts and Multimedia

English learners at the beginning level can read texts appropriate to their English level written by adults or other students. They can gain further understanding of a topic through field trips and multimedia technology such as audiotapes and video clips. This variety offers access to diverse learners, such as students with particular learning modality strengths (e.g., visual, auditory, spatial, kinesthetic; individual versus social learning).

Step 1. Identify key conceptual links and ideas to find texts at students' readability levels (with assistance as in Option 3).

Step 2. Depending on need, model the use of new technology. Technology and other interactive media may be introduced as part of the Explore, Explain or Elaborate Stages to support concept development. Front-load key conceptual ideas and key academic vocabulary in context as described in Option 3, with the addition of available interactive media.

Step 3. Provide options for students to access content and represent their understanding. Students choose reading and multimedia materials according to ability and personal interests. Students may produce portfolios and demonstrate understanding using a variety of media tools (e.g., slide shows, printed photos, flow charts, graphs).

Step 4. Students may be assigned to small groups, rotate through stations that include technology use, or work independently. Serve as facilitator and coach, consulting and conferencing with students individually or in small groups about their portfolio work.

SEVEN STRATEGIES FOR SCAFFOLDING SCIENCE LEARNING

The graphic to the right presents the sequence in which we describe each of the seven strategies to scaffold learning for English learners. Strategies 1–4 are primarily used in teacher activities — lectures and teacher-led student conversations:

1. **Visuals.** These include nonlinguistic representations (e.g., photos, models, realia) and graphic organizers that visually represent the relationships among ideas.

2. **Cues.** Cueing strategies consist of three types. **Hints** directly frame or preview the learning. **Questions** reinforce what has been taught and check for understanding. **Advance Organizers** orient students to upcoming important content.

3. **Think Aloud.** The teacher uses Think Aloud to verbalize his or her own thought processes while reading aloud, showing a video, or conducting an experiment, etc.

4. **KWL+.** The teacher starts a lesson by recording students' responses to questions about what they already know (K) and what they want to know (W). At the end of a lesson the teacher records what has been learned (L). The "+" aspect of KWL+ refers to the final step of making connections among the three categories of information.

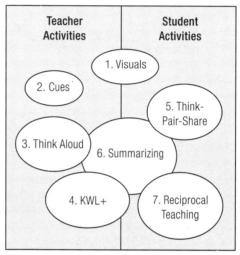

Strategies 5–7 are primarily student activities — the teacher guides students while they practice individual and team learning:

5. **Think-Pair-Share.** In Think-Pair-Share, the teacher poses a challenging, open-ended question and gives students one or two minutes to think; student pairs discuss their ideas, and then pairs share ideas with a larger group or the whole class.

6. **Summarizing.** In Summarizing, students must comprehend and distill information into a parsimonious, synthesized form — in their own words. **Note taking** is a form of summarizing that should follow a well-taught model.

7. **Reciprocal Teaching.** As a reading activity, in small groups, students follow a structured dialogue that involves four processes that good readers use — questioning, summarizing, clarifying, and predicting.

In the pages that follow, we describe each strategy, including some examples of how it may be combined with or embedded in other strategies. We encourage all teachers to look for ways to integrate these strategies into their science lessons. (Chapter 7 provides two detailed lessons that demonstrate integrated applications of these and the vocabulary tools introduced in the previous chapter.) Each strategy can be used in many, if not all, of the 5 Es stages; for instance, a graphic organizer (see Visuals) can be reused in the same form or with increasing elaboration as students review and build upon concepts and connections they have learned and discovered.

VISUALS, INCLUDING GRAPHIC ORGANIZERS

Purpose By generating mental pictures to go along with information, as well as by creating graphic representations for that information, students are putting the information to work, necessarily constructing meaning as they do so. The primary method of presenting new knowledge to students is in linguistic form — by using words. When teachers help students create nonlinguistic representations of new learning, as with pictures or symbols or by organizing information graphically, it increases students' opportunities to learn. The more that learners use both systems of representation, linguistic and nonlinguistic, the better they are able to think about and recall knowledge.

Description Visuals can be realia (real objects), models (e.g., molecules made from craft materials, sample research reports), demonstrations, pictures, illustrations, or videos and other visual media (e.g., webcasts, animations).

Graphic organizers are visual tools for recording and recalling important information. Organizers may have labels (words, phrases), illustrations, and use spatial orientation with lines or arrows to show organization and connections. Common graphic organizers include the following: KWL chart, flowchart, cause-and-effect map, matrix, classification map, spider (web) map, Venn diagram, T-chart, fishbone chart, and sequence of events.

Use Graphic organizers can be used for ELD or content area instruction and assessment. They can be used in conjunction with lecture and discussion; they can be embedded in the use of KWL charts and note taking. They can be useful learning and assessment tools, especially for early intermediate to intermediate English learners who are not yet adept at using complex grammar and function words to connect ideas in English. During learning, graphic organizers combine visual representation with oral discussion, helping English learners connect concepts. During assessment, graphic organizers help English learners show and communicate what they understand as an alternative to or in support of a long, complex response (e.g., many connected sentences) orally or in writing. A graphic organizer can help all students organize their thoughts before writing an essay or research report.

Examples A variety of websites and other resources feature graphic organizers, tools for generating graphic organizers, and student samples across a range of content areas. The examples offered below have valuable science applications.

DESCRIBING

Bubble Map

This simple format can be used to collect ideas or attributes, especially in a group or individual brainstorm. The teacher or students can suggest how to show the relationships among ideas.

VISUALS, INCLUDING GRAPHIC ORGANIZERS (CONTINUED)

Examples
(continued)

COMPARING AND CONTRASTING

Matrix

A matrix is especially useful for comparing a number of items across a number of distinctions or attributes.

Venn Diagram

Venn diagrams organize and compare sets of information. Enclosed shapes show ideas or characteristics that are unique and/or overlap for two or more topics.

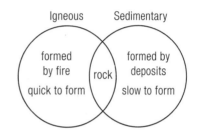

Igneous — formed by fire, quick to form

rock

Sedimentary — formed by deposits, slow to form

T-Chart

An idea or object is written at the top of the "T" and two contrasting sets of ideas are entered into each column.

Idea or Object	
Advantages	Disadvantages
Pro	Con
Fact	Opinion
Before	After

Black Holes	
What I thought	What I know now

CLASSIFYING AND CATEGORIZING

Spiderweb

"Legs" from the central idea (body) often are categories such as properties or characteristics of an object; lines from each leg are the important details, facts, instances, or other type of evidence to support and describe the category.

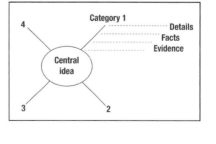

VISUALS, INCLUDING GRAPHIC ORGANIZERS (CONTINUED)

Examples
(continued)

Q&A Web

The teacher establishes major questions about an idea or object, preferably questions that have more than one answer; then students generate answers. Small groups might be assigned one question to work on together and report back to the class.

SEQUENCING

Sequence of Events

For describing an experiment, students can identify the beginning context, the procedural steps or causal observed chain reaction in an experiment, and report the result and their conclusion.

Cycle of Events

Each phase of a cycle, such as in an ecosystem or water cycle, may be identified with short phrases and supported with pictures or illustrations.

Hierarchy Web

This simple example of a hierarchy web for organisms wraps around to conserve space; an actual web with more complexity might descend a vertical axis with sublevels, features, examples, or other classification attributes in bubbles along horizontal lines.

VISUALS, INCLUDING GRAPHIC ORGANIZERS (CONTINUED)

Examples
(continued)

CAUSE AND EFFECT

Cause-and-Effect Web

Students can use a cause-and-effect web to describe investigations or experiments.

> *Investigation:* Identify the problem, relevant factors that (might) have an effect, one or more solutions, and the observed results and conclusion.

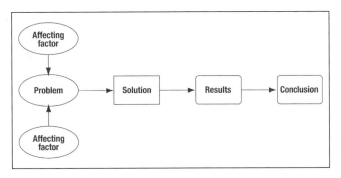

> *Experiment:* State the hypothesis and identify the independent variable and factors to control, list the procedural steps, and report the results and conclusion or inference.

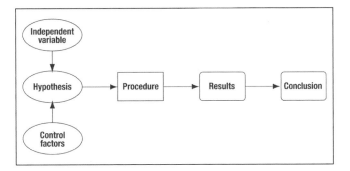

Fishbone Map

This graphic organizer depicts deductive reasoning, with an idea initiating the process toward a conclusion. Each pair of "fishbones" might represent a cause (above) with its observed effect (below). Another way to use the structure is to show a sequence (e.g., the missions to Mars in search of water), with dates and findings paired above and below along the way to a conclusion.

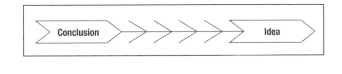

CUES

Purpose	Cues include **hints, advance organizers,** and **questions** that are used to focus student thinking and reasoning on pertinent information and help them build bridges among related concepts or chunks of information. All three approaches engage students in thinking by activating their prior knowledge and helping them organize it.
Description	The teacher provides cues as **hints** that directly frame or preview learning. Cues can be a reminder of how information was already presented, to guide students' recall and reasoning. Cues are often given to support English learners during questioning and presentation of an advance organizer. **Advance organizers** orient students to upcoming important content. They may take the form of an outline, skimming a chapter, or graphic organizers. Advance organizers bridge between what the student already knows and the material that will be taught next. Advance organizers can be embedded in the "K" or "know" part of a KWL+ chart.
	The teacher uses **questions** about what has already been taught to reinforce or check understanding about important information or when modeling procedures, such as predicting and hypothesizing. These questions may be used to elicit higher-order thinking processes such as summarizing, analyzing, and making inferences. These questions should not only be about basic factual information.
	Students use questions themselves to ask for clarification or indicate what they would like to learn, such as during the "W" or "what do you want to learn" part of a KWL+ chart. Students' questions can lead to class discussion that engages all students in listening to one another's thinking and offering ideas while practicing the use of academic language. Students' questions alert the teacher to what students know, do not know, or misunderstand. When a student's question reflects a misconception, it is an opportunity for further exploration, with the teacher guiding class discussion.
Use	In addition to the uses described above, cues are used as a prereading activity to build background knowledge or at the start of a lesson to alert students to what will be taught and to connect to their personal and prior learning context. Cues may be used in conjunction with teaching key vocabulary words, especially for English learners.
Example	As an advance organizer, the teacher draws a chart with three columns labeled "animal," "characteristic," and "function." The teacher checks for understanding by asking for definitions of the labels before proceeding. The teacher states that students will see a video and then read about how several animals use their senses. The teacher asks students to define senses. Before each animal on the video clip is presented, the teacher provides a cue about the animal's specialized sense organ by asking a question (e.g., "How does a snake see in complete darkness?"). After the video clip on snakes' infrared vision, the teacher provides cues as necessary for students to write notes in their charts. This might be a time to include think-pair-share.

CUES (CONTINUED)

Examples
(continued)

Animal	Characteristic Organ – Body part	Function Job of body part – What it does
Snake	Two "visual" organs: 1. Eyes 2. Heat-sensing pockets near eyes	Two types of "vision": 1. Eyesight like humans 2. Detects heat to "see" live objects in the dark
Ant	Antennae	Chemical sensor, similar to smell
Shark	Special long skin band on side of body	Senses electric and magnetic forces, motion, sound, and pressure

During the lesson, the teacher monitors pairs or small groups as they conduct experiments and write notes or fill in graphic organizers and answer questions. For groups needing assistance, the teacher asks probing and clarifying questions instead of providing easy answers. For example:

>> Suppose a snake did not have infrared sensors. What do you think would happen to the snake? (The teacher may need to give cues about a snake's desert environment and night hunting to focus on the function of sensors for survival.)

>> What is similar about the sensors of the animals? What is different? Why don't they have the same sensors?

>> Each animal lives in a different environment and has different sensors. What can you conclude from that?

THINK ALOUD

Purpose	The teacher uses think alouds to make scientific thinking transparent. Think alouds are used to teach comprehension skills, scaffold reading of difficult informational text, or model thought processes in an investigation or exploration. Think alouds can be used to explicitly connect text and visual concepts and express association, time sequence, or cause and effect. Think alouds are also used to verbalize a prediction, hypothesis, conclusion, or inductive or deductive inference.
Description	The teacher verbalizes his or her own thought processes while orally reading a science textbook, while showing a film clip, during each step of an experiment, or during a class discussion. The teacher orally models the interactive nature of comprehending a concept and scientific thinking. Think aloud may be used in conjunction with taking notes or constructing diagrams or graphic organizers. Think aloud makes "visible" the thinking processes, decisions, connections, and clarifications of actively trying to make meaning. Think aloud also is a way to model using the academic language of science before asking students to practice it in their conversations and writing.
Use	The teacher models out loud how a scientist thinks. The teacher also models out loud how a learner comprehends while reading a textbook, observing phenomena, conducting an experiment, or participating in a discussion. The teacher gradually fades out the modeling by stopping less often or providing less prompting, while fading in opportunities for students to practice thinking aloud.
	When students think aloud, the teacher may find that students observe the same phenomena but have different perceptions or arrive at different inferences. When students verbalize their thoughts and rationales, the teacher can "see" how they think, identify misconceptions or faulty reasoning, and guide them to proper scientific thinking.
Example	The teacher draws the structure of the organs and tissues involved in the process of vision. While drawing front and then side views of the eye, the teacher labels each part and then explains the function. The teacher may summarize at certain points, "What I know so far is…"
	Rather than just explain the process of vision from the eye to recognition in the brain, the teacher may pose questions or predictions at each step. Sentence frames may be included to support the teacher's oral questions, answers, and comments. To make the presentation more interactive, the teacher may pose questions and ask students to answer, adjusting explanations to address students' knowledge gaps or misunderstandings.

KWL+

Purpose Eliciting from students what they know and want to know, and then what they have learned about a topic serves to get students ready to construct new knowledge, build interest in the topic, and appreciate what they are learning. Student responses help the teacher adjust the lesson to fit students' needs, preconceptions, misconceptions, and interests and to monitor their understanding.

Description This is a reading-thinking strategy and tool. The teacher writes on a three-column chart students' responses to questions about what is already known (K) about the topic to be studied, what students want to know (W), and then what has been learned after the reading or lesson (L). In addition (+), the teacher draws lines or uses a graphic organizer to show connections among the recorded KWL information.

Use In advance of the reading or lesson, the teacher can check for individual understanding (K) by asking students to write or otherwise indicate their responses individually before asking for class responses. Any knowledge gaps or misunderstandings (e.g., personal, religious, or cultural beliefs not supported by science) that arise will alert the teacher to areas of the lesson needing special attention. Asking what students want to know (W) connects to their personal interests and builds motivation to learn more. Asking what students learned (L) allows them to consolidate their learning and identify gaps in knowledge they still have. Graphically mapping (+) this information helps to organize and connect ideas in the chart. The KWL+ chart can be used at all levels to review, predict, inquire, and summarize.

Example The teacher asks, "What do you know about light?" and writes students' responses in the "K" column of the KWL chart.

Then the teacher asks what students want to know about light and records their questions in the "W" column. At important points during the lesson, the teacher asks students what they just learned and enters responses in the "L" column. The teacher draws lines to connect old and new information to the inquiry questions and summarizes the connections (+ mapping). The "L" column might incorporate the results of note taking or graphic organizers. Information might be reorganized into categories or as main ideas and supporting details.

THINK-PAIR-SHARE

Purpose   Think-pair-share engages all students simultaneously. It gives students a chance to think about a question, share information with a partner, and consider a peer's point of view in a low-risk situation. This can be especially valuable for English learners and structures a way for them to rehearse for whole class participation. Students are typically more willing to respond in a whole class conversation after they have had a chance to discuss their ideas with a classmate.

Description   The teacher poses a challenging, open-ended question and gives students a minute or two to think about it and start to formulate an answer. Then, in pairs, students discuss their ideas for a few minutes. To protect the opportunity of partners to have equal speaking time, the teacher may want to set time limits and have partners trade speaking and listening roles at a given signal. After the partner discussions, the teacher invites partnership reports, randomly calls on students, or takes a classroom "vote."

Use   This strategy can be used to apply academic vocabulary, review and summarize what was taught or read, brainstorm ideas, or explore opinions. Pairing two English learners allows them to practice communication skills and learn in a low-anxiety context. When a more proficient English speaker works with a less proficient English speaker, there is also an opportunity for the students to benefit from their roles as English teacher and learner.

Example
» To begin exploration, students turn to their partners and each offers a prediction about an experiment or develops a concept; the teacher asks pairs to share unique predictions with the whole class.

» During data analysis, students analyze charts and graphs and pair-share their interpretations (e.g., "I think this graph means that …").

» At the end of an experiment, students pair-share their conclusions.

SUMMARIZING

Purpose Summarizing helps students understand complex information as they reorganize it for their own purposes. Summarizing can take place during a lecture as students take notes and during and after reading, investigations, or experiments as they seek to make sense of a body of new information. And because summaries identify key information, they help students review and study for tests.

Description Summarizing requires students to comprehend and distill information into a parsimonious, synthesized form, in their own words. To effectively summarize information, the learner must recognize the main ideas, the expendable details, the illuminating details, and the terminology or academic language that is a crucial aspect of communicating the content.

Note taking is closely related to summarizing, since to take effective notes, a student must determine what is most important and then state the information succinctly, in a way that will convey meaning for future use and review.

Use The primacy-recency effect states that people generally can remember the first and last parts of a long sequence, but not much from the middle. Summarization at each chunk of new information helps students perform a mental task of moving meaningful chunks to long-term memory.

The teacher begins teaching how to summarize and take notes by explaining the purpose and then modeling the process. Learning to summarize well is difficult, and so even secondary students can benefit from explicit practice, perhaps with the teacher providing writing prompts and templates that help students focus on the information that is most important. Novice English learners likely will need scaffolds such as sentence frames, graphic organizers, and illustrations. These can also be embedded in note-taking templates. It may be helpful for English learners to complete summaries and notes with the support of small groups.

Examples SAMPLE SENTENCE FRAMES
for beginning and early intermediate English learners:

Beginning

Some living things, or <u>organisms</u>, look the same, or <u>alike</u>. Some have bodies that work, or <u>function</u>, alike.

Organisms that <u>look</u> alike or that <u>work</u> alike share common characteristics. Scientists group organisms by <u>common characteristics</u>.

Groups are organized using a <u>classification</u> system. Scientists use <u>seven groups</u> to organize and study organisms. We call these groups <u>taxonomic categories</u>.

Early Intermediate

Groups of organisms can have similar <u>body plans</u> or similar <u>body functions</u>. These groups share <u>common characteristics</u>.

SUMMARIZING (CONTINUED)

Examples
(continued)

Scientists use a <u>classification system</u> to identify and <u>organize organisms</u> by their <u>characteristics</u>. There are seven groups, or <u>taxonomic categories</u>, to classify organisms.

NOTE-TAKING TEMPLATES

Window notes are a simple format for dividing note-taking space into categories. For a topic or time period, the teacher provides categories, or windowpanes, into which students can organize information. Here is an example from a middle school science teacher who uses a variety of window notes that help students organize and summarize information.

Illustrations with labels	Vocabulary
Key concepts	Questions

In the Cornell method of note taking, a sheet of paper is divided into three parts and a student uses the five R's: First, the student **records** notes of important facts or concepts in the main body; these are "telegraphic sentences" that succinctly state an important idea. Second, the student **reduces** the information to questions or cues in a two-inch column. Third, the student covers the recorded notes and uses the cues to **recite** as much information as possible, perhaps as homework review. Fourth, the student **reflects** on what was learned and summarizes the most important facts or opinions at the bottom of the page. Fifth, the student uses the completed template at any time for quick **review.**

Record (1)	Reduce (2)	Recite (3)
Reflect (4)		Review (5)

For example, students work in pairs or triads on an experiment and record procedures and data results at each step in their own notebooks using the Cornell method. Beginning English learners are given note templates with sentence frames. The teacher monitors group work, checks for correct and complete concepts in the notes, and asks prompting questions to guide learning and note taking. The teacher models and helps certain students formulate cues. Homework assignments include adding reflection statements and reviewing notes.

RECIPROCAL TEACHING

Purpose	Students learn specific reading comprehension skills by practicing them explicitly in small groups.
Description	Reciprocal teaching is an interactive, structured dialogue during the reading of text. It involves four processes that good readers use — **questioning, summarizing, clarifying,** and **predicting.** These four processes are also core scientific thinking processes; so reciprocal teaching capitalizes on investigation and experimentation standards in science. First, the teacher models the dialogue process; then pairs or small groups of students assume the roles of discussion leader and discussant(s).
Use	The teacher models one or more of the four processes with a short segment of the text, then asks students to practice a cycle of reciprocal teaching in pairs or triads. The teacher models again with a second, longer segment for another cycle of reciprocal teaching. The teacher continues to gradually lengthen the segment that is used. While students conduct reciprocal teaching, the teacher monitors and intervenes when necessary. Initially the teacher provides intensive modeling and scaffolding and gradually fades out these prompts. For groups needing more assistance, the teacher continues to model. Summarizing is especially difficult for students to master. Additional practice, including practice with note taking, may be appropriate. Word walls and sample sentence frames can help English learners use academic language and participate in groups' reciprocal teaching conversations.

Example	The teacher gives student groups the following questions to answer during or after reading text about the causes and consequences of global warming.
	
	Question
	After students read the selection, one student in the group asks another to answer a meaningful comprehension question.
	
	    "What is the greenhouse effect?"
	
	    "How does the greenhouse effect relate to global warming?"
	
	Summarize
	One student asks another to paraphrase the important points or concepts in the reading.
	
	    "Please summarize in your own words what we have just read."
	
	Clarify
	Group members discuss any confusing aspects of the reading and try to make connections to knowledge they already have.
	
	    "What does it mean that energy from the sun gets absorbed? How does that work?"
	
	    "If the temperature of the earth is rising anyway, why should we worry about it? Isn't that what is supposed to happen?"
	
	Predict/Hypothesize
	Students use new knowledge to make a hypothesis.
	
	    "I hypothesize that if CO_2 emissions and other gases are the cause of the rise in greenhouse gases, restrictions on the use of sources of CO_2 emissions will lower greenhouse gases."
	
	    "I predict that if we reduce greenhouse gases fast, the effect of global warming will be reduced just as fast."

ENDNOTES FOR CHAPTER 5

[1] Scaffolding is discussed widely in education literature. The following sources are particularly germane to this presentation of scaffolding science instruction for English learners:

Ellis, E.S., & Worthington, L.A. (2004). Executive summary of the research synthesis on effective teaching principles and the design of quality tools for educators. Retrieved Feb. 1, 2006, from http://idea.uoregon.edu/~ncite/documents/techrep/tech05.pdf.

Fitzgerald, J. & Graves, M.F. (2004). *Scaffolding reading experiences for English-language learners* (p. 16). Norwood, MA: Christopher-Gordon Publishers.

Freeman, D. & Freeman, Y. (1988). Sheltered English instruction. ERIC Clearinghouse on Languages and Linguistics, Washington, DC. *ERIC Digest* (ED301070). Retrieved March 3, 2006, from http://www.ericdigests.org/pre-9210/english.htm.

Galguera, T. (2003). Scaffolding for English learners: What's a science teacher to do? *Quality teaching for English learners: Module 6. Teaching science to adolescent English learners.* San Francisco: WestEd.

National Clearinghouse on Bilingual Education (1987). Sheltered English: An approach to content area instruction for limited-English-proficient students. *Forum, 10*(6), 1–3.

Walqui, A. (2003). Quality Teaching for Secondary English Learners workshop materials. San Francisco: WestEd. See http://www.wested.org/cs/we/view/serv/33.

[2] Gibbons, P. (2002) *Scaffolding language, scaffolding learning.* Portsmouth, NH: Heinemann.

[3] See, for example, the resources that follow:

Marzano, R.J., Pickering, D.J., & Pollock, J.E. (2001). *Classroom instruction that works: Research-based strategies for increasing student achievement.* Alexandria, VA: Association for Supervision and Curriculum Development.

California Department of Education (2000). *Strategic teaching and learning: Standards-based instruction to promote content literacy in grades four through twelve.* Sacramento: California Department of Education Press.

CISC Science Subcommittee (2002). *Strategic science teaching.* Sacramento: California Department of Education, Curriculum and Instruction Steering Committee of the California County Superintendents Educational Services Association.

Herrell, A.L., & Jordan, M.L. (2003). *Fifty strategies for teaching English language learners.* Englewood Cliffs, NJ: Prentice Hall.

[4] Lee, O. (2005). Science education with English language learners: Synthesis and research agenda. *Review of Educational Research, 75,* 491–530.

CHAPTER 6

Assessing English Learners

Science teachers who focus on giving English learners equal access to the curriculum will also want to make sure that these students have a reasonable way to communicate what they are learning. Equal assessment opportunity for English learners means lowering language barriers in the testing process so that the focus is on science learning, not mastery of English.

This chapter discusses how to select, modify, and administer good classroom assessments that inform a teacher about English learners' true understanding of science content. The heart of this chapter describes a variety of accommodations that can make classroom assessments fair for English learners. These accommodations maintain a focus on the same content standards for all students while offering students different ways of performing on the assessment that respect their differences and yield accurate results for all students.

THE "SCIENCE" OF ASSESSMENT

Assessing students at the end of each study unit or chapter — summative assessment — informs the teacher and student of final levels of accomplishment and allows the teacher to analyze results for groups of students (e.g., girls, English learners) as well as for individuals. Information about who struggled to understand and what they failed to understand informs the teacher's decisions about how to modify the teaching strategies and activities for the next lesson or to offer program interventions such as tutoring. But how can the teacher greatly reduce the number of students who fail to understand by the end of the unit? Summative assessment is not enough. In support of summative assessment, formative assessment, particularly informal techniques to check for understanding before the start of a lesson and repeatedly during a lesson, is the key to effective teaching and learning.

The National Research Council frames such assessment as the process of teaching scientifically:

> Teachers collect information about students' understanding almost continuously and make adjustments to their teaching on the basis of their interpretation of that information. They observe critical incidents in the classroom, formulate hypotheses about the causes of those incidents, question students to test their hypotheses, interpret students' responses, and adjust their teaching plans.[1]

In these terms, assessment allows the teacher to treat each lesson as an experiment, predicting that certain strategies and activities will help students learn rigorous content, monitoring the effects of the lesson on student engagement and achievement, and analyzing the assessment data to make conclusions about teaching practices and materials.

Formative assessment can be a powerful teaching tool when teachers use the results to adjust their instructional strategies to reach all students in the classroom.[2] As Benjamin Bloom found, teachers using formative assessment dramatically narrowed the range of student achievement (test scores) and the average student outperformed 84 percent (instead of the expected 50 percent) of students in traditional classrooms where the teachers did not make instructional adjustments.[3] In other words, when teachers take the time to assess as they teach, and use the feedback, the process can result in more students mastering the lesson content.

The effective teacher uses a few quick and easy methods to survey what students do and do not understand during the course of a lesson and then tries different approaches as needed. Just as an ounce of prevention is worth a pound of cure, noticing early failures to comprehend key ideas and adjusting a lesson to fit student needs can prevent many failures at the end of the unit of study.

Three techniques to check for understanding during a lesson are gaining in popularity among elementary, middle school, and high school teachers:

>> hand gestures such as thumbs up (I agree, yes), thumbs to the side (I politely disagree, no), and flat hand over the head (I do not understand the question or comment);

>> color-coded cards — agree, disagree, don't understand; and

>> white boards on which each student quickly illustrates or writes a brief answer and holds it up for the teacher to see.

These techniques can be used to respond to what the teacher or another student says. Asking all students to quickly show agreement or disagreement with another student's answer or comment engages all students in listening critically to one another and widens the conversation from teacher–student to teacher–student–students. Students easily adapt to these techniques, and the process is both fast and comfortable. And the teacher can take immediate action based on what the students reveal. For example, a concept about which many students signal confusion indicates to the teacher the need to take a different approach; if a smaller group of students signal that they do not understand, the teacher may convene them for reteaching while other students move into an independent activity.

Monitoring students while they are working individually or in small groups can be considered checking for understanding. The teacher is able to observe many students and provide cues or other teaching techniques to guide individual students in their learning activities. When many students are confused, the teacher may stop the independent work and conduct direct instruction to clarify concepts or the learning activity itself. This is what makes a good teacher really effective — planning a good lesson and then making it better during instruction so all students can be successful.

ASSESSMENT ACCOMMODATIONS FOR ENGLISH LEARNERS

Accommodations are meant to elicit the most accurate information about what students know and can do without giving them an unfair advantage over students who do not receive the accommodations. All students are diverse test-takers as well as diverse learners. Some may have pronounced learning strengths in certain modalities, such as visual or aural, or they may have assessment preferences that influence their ability to show what they truly know. For English learners, an additional consideration is the challenge they face to perform in English. The more alternatives an assessment includes, the more accurate the test results are likely to be for a range of students.

Figure 6.1 describes common testing accommodations that teachers may use in their classrooms with English learners. It is assumed that testing is in English only. Some accommodations address how a test is administered; others address the test instrument and task options. The closer an English learner is to the beginning ELD level, the more scaffolding of the student's interaction with the test will be required.

ACCOMMODATIONS BY TYPE OF ASSESSMENT

The particular accommodations the teacher decides to use with English learners will vary by the type of assessment as well as by the student's level of English proficiency. Several kinds of assessments that teachers commonly use are described below, along with suggestions to accommodate English learners.

Cloze Test

Cloze tests are similar to sentence frames. They require students to fill in the blanks in sentences with key words. Sometimes a word bank may be provided but, if so, it should include extra words and/or allow for words to be used more than once. The point is to reduce student guessing; the teacher needs to be fairly certain what students do and do not know to confidently plan what to teach next.

>> Ensure that all words in a sentence are familiar to English learners so that the assessment is testing only students' knowledge of the intended terms — those represented with blanks.

>> For beginning and early intermediate students, modify sentences to be as simple as possible and to help students with the reading.

FIGURE 6.1. Test Accommodations for Use With English Learners

Test Accommodation	Purpose or Use
Extra Time	Provide extra time for English learners to read and understand test questions. They have extra thinking to do simply to understand and respond to a question in English.
Word Walls, Glossaries, Dictionaries	Provide word walls created during instruction for reference during assessment so English learners can more easily communicate conceptual thinking. Allow English learners at appropriate ELD levels to use glossaries and English and/or bilingual dictionaries (except when testing vocabulary, naturally).
Notes in Primary Language	When students are allowed to use notes during an assessment, allow English learners to refer to notes they made in their primary language. In this way the teacher makes it more likely that students can produce, in English, answers that they know in their primary language.
Models and Rubrics	Provide models of expected student work, particularly for students who have not previously produced this kind of product. Preview the scoring guide or rubric that will be used to judge the work. Previewing models and explaining rubrics before or during instruction helps students understand lesson and assessment objectives.
Enhanced Test Directions	Some test directions can be much more difficult to understand than the concepts measured. Read directions aloud and rephrase them as necessary to be sure English learners know what they are expected to do. Simplify test directions as much as possible. For example, segment multi-step directions if possible, stating one step at a time and allowing for student response between steps. When responses cannot be segmented, have students use the directions as a checklist for reviewing that they have completed all parts of the task.
Enhanced Test Items	Ensure that English learners encounter in a test the same key words and phrases that were used during instruction. Increase students' opportunity to understand the questions by providing synonyms or additional context for key ideas.
Oral Responses	Communicating through writing can be very challenging for English learners, especially when anxiety is high during an assessment. Allow novice English learners to give oral responses while the rest of the class completes a written test. (Out of range of the rest of the class, prompt students individually and scaffold the conversation as necessary to elicit meaningful responses.) Provide English learners who need support with sentence frames for open-ended questions and ask them to attempt written answers; then prompt students orally to give them an opportunity to clarify written answers that are ambiguous or confusing.
Illustrations, Graphic Organizers	Allow students to express ideas with labeled drawings, diagrams, or graphic organizers. Follow up by asking students to give oral explanations, written open-ended responses, or demonstrations.
Hands-on Activities	Have students perform a demonstration, activity, or experiment, and describe or explain their actions and thinking processes. For example, students might cycle through various assessment task stations in the lab, responding to the problem or question posed at each station. Have students who can write brief answers do so, and orally prompt English learners as needed.
Language Conventions	Ignore errors in language conventions in order to focus on students' understanding of science content. The time for corrective feedback of oral or written responses is during instruction. Expect beginning and early intermediate English learners to make many errors as they struggle to communicate meaning.
Small Groups	Administer a test separately to a small group of English learners if it helps to lower their anxiety (students still individually complete the test). Use prompts and scaffolds with individuals in the group and allow oral responses as appropriate to elicit students' best performance.

Multiple-Choice Test

Multiple-choice tests can be very difficult for English learners since the test items are typically very succinct — with little context to help English learners figure out what an item means. Teachers may need to support English learners by rephrasing and providing context clues for certain test items.

>> Spend a little time teaching test-taking skills, particularly related to science. If some test items require students to pick the "best" answer, ensure that English learners understand and have had experience with this type of item. Let them know that there may be answers that are partially correct but just not as good as the "most correct" or "best" answer.

>> Limit the number of items, especially items with long statements, to avoid student fatigue.

>> Eliminate items with answer choices such as "None of the above" and "A and B" to avoid confusion and cognitive overload.

>> Make sure item stems and answer choices are written in the simplest, most straightforward wording possible. Highlight key words (in bold, underline, or all capital letters), particularly negatives such as "not," so English learners do not miss them.

For multiple-choice tests that base items on illustrations, graphs, or tables, the following tips are helpful for all learners and are especially important to avoid confusing English learners.[4]

>> Make sure illustrations are accurate and clear and include appropriate scales when relevant.

>> Use the illustration as a reference for multiple questions. English learners will benefit from the familiar context.

>> Be sure the labels on the illustration match those embedded in item prompts.

>> Limit the steps necessary to interpret information from an illustration, graph, or table.

>> When possible, select contexts that are familiar to students or that relate to their backgrounds and experiences.

Short-Answer Test

Students can respond orally or in writing to test items calling for a phrase or up to a few sentences. When applicable, students may be encouraged to draw illustrations or to create or fill in simple graphic organizers (e.g., to show a cause–effect relationship), organizing their thoughts before answering aloud or in writing. Short-answer tests can be structured to provide sentence starters and function words to connect ideas, with the amount of support matching students' ELD levels.

>> For beginning English learners, conduct the test orally, individually, and out of range of the rest of the class. Use visual supports without "giving away" answers, particularly for English learners whose strong modality is visual or spatial.

>> For early intermediate English learners, conduct the test orally or orally prompt for certain items that students may have had trouble answering in writing. Word walls and sentence frames support students to communicate what they know.

>> Intermediate English learners can answer in writing but may need supports such as word walls and sentence frames.

Written Performance Tasks

The writing students do in science varies across types, purposes, and products. For example, students write expository, descriptive, analytic, and technical forms. They write for purposes such as exemplifying, describing phenomena, raising questions, clarifying, and supporting ideas. And they create different types of products such as notes, portfolios, data charts, reports, essays, and scientific logs.

Students need explicit teaching about the purpose and form of each type of writing. Such instruction by the science teacher can be supported with collaboration from the English language arts or ELD teacher. For all students, models should be a key feature of science writing instruction. Models should be discussed with students and available for them to investigate and refer to. Graphic organizers can be used with students to get their thinking organized. Word walls, of course, should be readily available to English learners.

The teacher should elicit student writing at all ELD levels but with different expectations depending on a student's English proficiency.

>> Beginning level English learners may give brief oral answers and perhaps also attempt to write a few simple phrases or sentences.

>> Early intermediate level English learners may write a few simple sentences followed by oral responses prompted by the teacher.

>> Intermediate level English learners may write sentences and short paragraphs and then clarify them orally as prompted by the teacher.

>> Early advanced and advanced English learners should be expected to produce paragraphs and compositions; the teacher is aware that language convention errors are still natural as students continue learning English grammar and idioms.

Figure 6.2 is an example of a written science assessment that gives English learners an opportunity to express their understanding at varying levels of language development. The assessment content is aligned with content standards relating to properties of matter and changes in the state of matter. Students approach the topic through three scaffolded items: explaining processes in an illustration, selecting academic language from key vocabulary on the word wall or test form to describe these processes, and applying knowledge of the processes in an open-ended writing task.[5]

The first part of the assessment includes the following components:

1. an illustration with labels to serve as reference for the entire assessment;

2. two example responses; and

3. Cloze-response prompts in the form of sentence frames with key vocabulary highlighted in bold letters.

The next part of the assessment example includes a diagram that identifies components in the system and their relationship to one another through the use of arrows. It also provides scaffolds for English learners as follows:

4. a vocabulary key to be applied in this new context;

5. an embedded example response; and

6. a graphic organizer with missing information to be completed.

The final part of the assessment is an open-ended question. To differentiate for English learners at early intermediate/intermediate levels, more support would be added by rephrasing the directions and providing a sentence starter.

7. an open-ended question or sentence starter.

Oral Presentations

Beginning or early intermediate English learners should not be required to present formal oral reports in mainstream classrooms; modified presentations might be appropriate in sheltered classrooms (where all students are English learners). Intermediate students might give presentations if modified to fit their communication levels, the students agree, and classroom conditions are risk-free and supportive. Multimedia and use of technology such as PowerPoint, where visuals are blended with brief text, can support English learners as they orally present their reports.

When English learners work in cooperative groups on a task culminating in an oral presentation, reporting in front of the class should be assigned to other students, while English learners are gradually prepared to participate more fully in oral presentations.

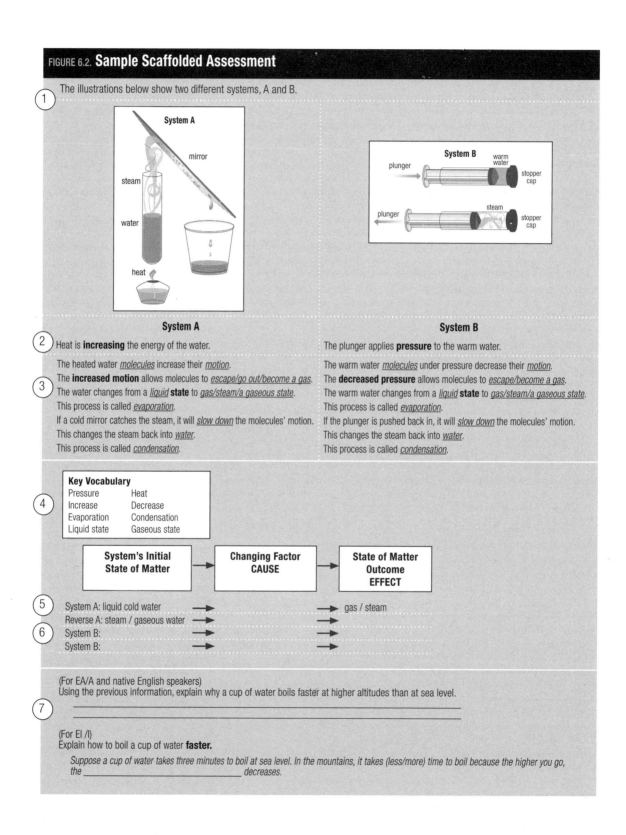

FIGURE 6.2. **Sample Scaffolded Assessment**

(1) The illustrations below show two different systems, A and B.

System A
steam
mirror
water
heat

System B
plunger — warm water — stopper cap
plunger — steam — stopper cap

System A	**System B**
(2) Heat is **increasing** the energy of the water.	The plunger applies **pressure** to the warm water.
(3) The heated water _molecules_ increase their _motion_. The **increased motion** allows molecules to _escape/go out/become a gas_. The water changes from a _liquid_ **state** to _gas/steam/a gaseous state_. This process is called _evaporation_. If a cold mirror catches the steam, it will _slow down_ the molecules' motion. This changes the steam back into _water_. This process is called _condensation_.	The warm water _molecules_ under pressure decrease their _motion_. The **decreased pressure** allows molecules to _escape/become a gas_. The warm water changes from a _liquid_ **state** to _gas/steam/a gaseous state_. This process is called _evaporation_. If the plunger is pushed back in, it will _slow down_ the molecules' motion. This changes the steam back into _water_. This process is called _condensation_.

(4)
Key Vocabulary
Pressure	Heat
Increase	Decrease
Evaporation	Condensation
Liquid state	Gaseous state

System's Initial State of Matter	**Changing Factor CAUSE**	**State of Matter Outcome EFFECT**

(5) System A: liquid cold water ⟶ ⟶ gas / steam
Reverse A: steam / gaseous water ⟶ ⟶
(6) System B: ⟶ ⟶
System B: ⟶ ⟶

(For EA/A and native English speakers)
Using the previous information, explain why a cup of water boils faster at higher altitudes than at sea level.

(7) _____

_____

(For EI /I)
Explain how to boil a cup of water **faster.**

_Suppose a cup of water takes three minutes to boil at sea level. In the mountains, it takes (less/more) time to boil because the higher you go, the _____ decreases._

Performance Assessments

Performing standards-based scientific investigations and experiments is a central strand of the National Science Education Standards. The use of investigations and experiments as assessment tools is a prime example of how assessment and instruction can blend together.[6] In performing an investigation as an assessment, students are asked to analyze a problem and generate a series of questions to be investigated. Then students design and conduct their investigation and organize and write a report.

INTEGRATING INSTRUCTION AND ASSESSMENT

In standards-based lesson planning, also called backwards mapping, the teacher first selects specific content standards as the lesson objectives, choosing a few of the most important or essential standards to discuss with students so they know to focus on these. The teacher, meanwhile, remains aware of the full complement of standards so as to make connections to them as appropriate.

Second, the teacher selects a good summative assessment that emphasizes those essential standards and then builds in accommodations for English learners. The teacher is aware of the test format and the vocabulary, knowledge, and skills required to answer the questions and follow the test directions. If possible, the teacher offers alternatives, knowing that diverse learners also prefer diverse ways to show what they have learned. The teacher asks several questions in evaluating an assessment:

>> Does the assessment truly measure (at least) the essential standards?

>> What will proficient performance on this assessment look like?

>> Do the accommodations for English learners really measure the science content standards at a reasonable rigor, as for other students?

Third, the teacher plans learning activities so that all students have equal opportunity to learn the content and practice the skills. Equal opportunity means that diverse learning activities are presented to students because they have diverse styles, interests, and levels of learning. Visual learners, for example, have graphic organizers and other visual means to access content, but they also experience other modalities to become well-rounded learners and appreciate a variety of styles within the classroom. Reading materials are geared to students' various reading levels. Students are able to choose from alternative tasks, which leads them to become more responsible for their own learning. In selecting the learning activities, the teacher reflects on each and asks whether it helps students understand the essential standards and prepares them for the assessment.

Fourth, the teacher plans instructional strategies and builds in differentiation, or scaffolds, for English learners at different ELD levels. Instruction is multimodal, perhaps focusing on a particular mode at one time and reviewing what was learned by focusing on another mode. Accommodations such as use of graphic organizers that appear in the assessment are part of the instructional strategies. The teacher evaluates the instructional strategies in light of whether they try to reach and respect the diversity of learners in the classroom and are linked to the assessment strategies.

Last, the teacher connects the dots by reviewing the entire unit lesson plan. What is taught is assessed. There must be a clear connection among the standards, assessment, student activities, and teaching strategies. If not, the teacher amends the lesson plan. During instruction, the teacher uses frequent formative assessments, checking for understanding and using the feedback to quickly adjust the lesson and try other strategies.

SHARING RESULTS AND IDEAS

A teacher can learn much from assessments or test results but still miss some things or not know how to help some students who are struggling. Collaborating with other teachers to evaluate student work or analyze test results can enhance both student and teacher learning.

The shared evaluation of student work might start with a trusted colleague and expand to departmental study teams. These sessions enable teachers to become more skilled at evaluating student work by giving them the opportunity to review and analyze a larger sample of work than that of their own students. By sharing results, teachers can also evaluate their individual programs and instructional practices in comparison with those of their peers.

While analyzing student results together, collaborating teachers also consider what they might do better the next time. They take a hard look at the results for lower-scoring students to determine whether the test was accurate and fair for these students. They also explore different teaching strategies and learning activities that might better help these students as a group, and they share insights about individual students. This kind of embedded professional development is highly relevant to teachers and can produce valuable results for students.

ENDNOTES FOR CHAPTER 6

[1] National Research Council (1996). *National Science Education Standards* (p. 87). Washington, DC: National Academy Press. Retrieved February 26, 2006, from http://www.nap.edu/catalog/4962.html.

[2] Black, P., & Wiliam, D. (1998). Inside the black box: Raising standards through classroom assessment. *Phi Delta Kappan, 80*(2), 139–149.

[3] Bloom, B. (1984). The search for methods of group instruction as effective as one-to-one tutoring. *Educational Leadership, 41*(8), 4–17.

[4] Sexton, U., & Solano-Flores, G. (2002, April). *Cultural validity in assessment: A cross-cultural study of the interpretation of mathematics and science test items*. Paper presented at the annual meeting of the American Educational Research Association, New Orleans.

[5] Ibid.

[6] Two publications give practical advice and examples about using investigations and experiments as performance assessments:

Fathman, A.K., & Crowther, D.T. (Eds.). (2005). *Science for English language learners: K–12 classroom strategies*. Arlington: VA: National Science Teachers Association Press.

Olson, S., & Loucks-Horsley, S. (Eds.) (2000). *Inquiry and the National Science Education Standards: A guide for teaching and learning*. Washington, DC: National Academies Press.

CHAPTER 7

Applying Strategies in the Classroom

This chapter pulls together many of the ideas introduced in the previous chapters, putting them into practice in two lesson scenarios. The scenarios show how teachers might plan for and integrate a number of key strategies and tools to differentiate instruction for their English learner students.

The first scenario goes inside a series of grade 9 Earth science lessons on the rock cycle. It highlights in particular the integration of graphic organizers and other visuals. The second scenario excerpts a grade 6 lesson on soils, highlighting how a teacher differentiates language use in dialogues and writing for two levels of English learners.

Even though good practice recommends placing beginning English learners in sheltered classrooms, sometimes they are placed in regular classrooms. This chapter assumes that teachers may find themselves with the full range of English learners, from beginning to advanced, mixed with students who are native English speakers.

Both lessons are set within the 5 Es cycle of engage, explore, explain, elaborate, and evaluate, and both benefit from a planning process similar to the one below.

PLANNING FOR DIFFERENTIATED INSTRUCTION

The steps in planning lessons differentiated for English learners are described below in the voice of a grade 9 teacher as she plans for a series of lessons on the rock cycle in Earth science.

As she plans, she identifies the following standards and essential questions and considers the class composition and grouping needs.

Key National Science Education Standards

Grades 5–8 Content Standard D (focus on the structure of the Earth system and the Earth's history)

Grades 9–12 Content Standard D (focus on matter, energy, crystal dynamics, cycles, geochemical processes, and expanded time scales)

The study of the Earth's energy sources as driving mechanisms of ongoing change facilitates deeper understanding of the evolution of the Earth system over geologic time. The cyclical nature of the formation and movement of materials (e.g., tectonism, rock and geochemical cycles) and the change in physical and chemical properties of the reservoirs of matter held within the Earth (e.g., molecules of silica in volcanic material and rocks, carbon, nitrogen, oxygen, and complex molecules that control the chemistry of life) are evidence of its dynamics.

This scenario fits within a larger conceptual framework of interactions among the solid earth, the oceans, the atmosphere, their yielding life, and the long-term stability and dynamic equilibrium resulting from the ongoing evolutionary changes of the Earth system.

Essential Questions

>> What drives the changes on the face of the Earth?

>> Is there any feature of the Earth that does not change?

>> Are these changes related, and how have they affected our planet? Our lives?

>> How do scientists use the evidence found in rocks (e.g., origin, structures, placement and forming processes) to better understand the dynamic Earth systems?

>> What is the significance of plate tectonics?

Class Composition and Grouping

In this grade 9 class of 30 students, 10 are English learners. Two are at the beginning ELD level, two are at the early intermediate level, four are intermediate, and two are early advanced. I generally make heterogeneous grouping assignments, but I often try to include a pair of English learners who speak the same language in a group. For some activities, I work separately with the beginning and early intermediate students.

Steps in Planning

This year, our high school science department decided to teach the science program using the Earth systems approach, integrating study of the biosphere, atmosphere, and lithosphere. This allows us to emphasize conceptual connections within and across disciplines and to bring in many real-world applications and issues in science and technology.

These lessons on the rock cycle take place toward the beginning of the school year, so my English learners need a great deal of scaffolded instruction. One-third of my 30 students in this class are English learners, at four levels of English language development.

I have a clear picture in my mind of the overarching concepts and key high school science standards the students will be expected to understand, as well as how they will demonstrate understanding on assessments.

IDENTIFY STANDARDS

I begin my planning by reviewing the state and national science standards that we will be covering. The big ideas of these lessons focus on the lithosphere, with a conceptual overview of the scale, structure, and dynamics of the Earth's crust in the process of rock formation. This series of lessons serves as a springboard from middle school science, preparing students for our 9–12 curriculum.

SELECT SUMMATIVE ASSESSMENT

In backwards mapping, after I select key standards as the focus of instruction and assessment, I select the summative assessment for the lesson series — in this case, I have chosen the textbook unit assessment — and I will modify it as necessary to fit my English learners.

PLAN INSTRUCTIONAL EXPERIENCES

Knowing what I will assess (the key standards) and how I will assess students (the assessment formats, directions, and accommodations for English learners), I plan differentiated instructional activities and teaching strategies so all students will have an equal opportunity to learn what will be assessed. I plan a variety of activities to engage all of the diverse learners in my class as they engage, explore, explain, elaborate, and evaluate. Students will have universal access to the curriculum through activities that are multimodal (students hear, see, speak, feel, perform), that repeat and spiral concepts, that gradually build academic language, and that use meaningful experiments and investigations in which students link concepts, answer specific questions, and ask their own questions. I see my role in large part to be that of facilitator of student-centered learning.

I also look for interdisciplinary connections as well as particular concepts that my students likely do not know but must learn as foundation knowledge. I anticipate the prior knowledge, cultural beliefs, and possible misconceptions that different students may bring to the lessons. Working with English learners, it is often necessary to embed some basic science experiences and much extra language development to help them meet grade-level expectations.

SELECT INSTRUCTIONAL MATERIALS

I need to find or modify print and Internet text sources to supplement the textbook for my English learners, especially those who are below the early advanced level, as well as for other students who struggle to read grade-level texts. In addition to text materials, I also use rocks and other realia, photos and illustrations, video clips, and a whole range of graphic organizers. I know that graphic organizers and other visuals are an important help for English learners as well as for other visual-spatial learners.

PLAN INSTRUCTIONAL STRATEGIES

In selecting instructional strategies, I incorporate many instructional "routines" since these predictable strategies especially benefit English learners. I select strategies to teach academic language and strategies to scaffold science learning. I also plan how I will use assessments. A 5 Es organizer is a good checklist for getting started (see figure 7.1).

FIGURE 7.1. 5 Es Organizer

Tool/Strategy	Engage	Explore	Explain	Elaborate	Evaluate
Text Sources by Reading Level				●	●
Teaching the Language of Scientists					
Vocabulary Self-Rating Sheet	●		●		
Concept Organizer			●		
Word Form Chart				●	
List-Group-Label					
Features Matrix				●	●
Word Wall, Glossary	●	●			
Sentence Frames			●	●	●
Scaffolding Science Learning					
Visuals, Graphic Organizers	●	●	●	●	●
Cues, Questions, Advance Organizers	●	●	●		
KWL +	●				
Think Aloud		●	●		
Think-Pair-Share	●	●	●		
Reciprocal Teaching					
Summarizing and Note Taking			●	●	
Assessing English Learners					
Word Wall	●	●	●	●	
Performance Accommodations				●	●

Gradually, as the unit unfolds and the English learners become familiar with the use of their science notebooks and other instructional routines, they will not need as much support. I will monitor their progress and adjust my level of support accordingly.

I also think about types of instruction appropriate to the learning activities in each of the 5 Es — whether I am going to be directing the instruction, facilitating it, or grouping students for peer-assisted activities. For each instance of grouping, I have to plan whether to allow students to select partners or groups, or, if assigning groups, what criteria to use — including English language proficiency, science literacy, learning styles, and personality.

Finally, I outline the activity sequence within a specific time frame and review the strategies that will support my English learners each step of the way (see figure 7.2).

FIGURE 7.2. Differentiating for English Learners

While the examples below refer in their specifics to a series of lessons about the rock cycle, the strategies for differentiating instruction and assessment apply universally.

Use **controlled speech.** Talk more slowly, break down very complex statements and questions into simpler sentences, and avoid idioms English learners do not know.

>> The teacher repeats and rephrases oral instruction and uses physical gestures, visuals, and other ways to clarify meaning, particularly to help English learners visualize abstract concepts (such as crystallization).

>> The teacher builds conceptual knowledge from simple statements to expanded and more complex statements and from focused examples and specific topics to interrelated and multidisciplinary connections.

Support oral instruction with **visuals,** particularly **graphic organizers,** and connect to observations, hands-on experiments, texts at different reading levels, and student notes.

>> Students observe demonstrations and conduct investigations at stations to compare and relate rock characteristics (that they can observe) to information on charts, matching rock type and potential formation process and location.

>> Students design and conduct an experiment, manipulate and analyze models, interpret data, and relate prior knowledge to new information.

>> Students organize, connect, and explain ideas with manipulatives, such as movable cards and arrows.

>> Students research information to support their conclusions.

Teach **vocabulary** within the context of the lesson, building from personal, informal definitions to expanded, formal definitions.

>> Students communicate understanding of Earth's natural hazards with peers, using images, video, and web-based models and information.

>> Students explore an epsom salt crystal-growing lab, with temperature gradient variables, and igneous, sedimentary, and metamorphic rock formation models.

>> Students use **vocabulary self-rating** to identify key words/terms they already know and new words that will need to be emphasized during the lesson.

Use **think aloud** to **model** scientific thinking and reading strategies and to clarify meaning.

>> The teacher thinks aloud whiile reading a text (e.g., locating key information, summarizing key ideas, predicting next steps or outcomes).

>> The teacher thinks aloud while demonstrating the experimental methodology.

>> The teacher models expectations for students' use of academic language during group discussions at stations so students are clear about how to discuss and take notes during investigations.

Use **word walls** as a learning tool for building vocabulary and as a reference chart when students speak and write throughout a series of lessons. (Word walls may also take the form of a series of overhead transparencies that students reproduce in personal glossaries.)

>> The teacher enhances word walls by organizing words (e.g., by characteristics), by including example sentences and synonyms/antonyms, and by supporting with pictures or illustrations.

>> The teacher provides students with multiple opportunities to practice using the new words in their speech and writing.

FIGURE 7.2. **Differentiating for English Learners (continued)**

Model **note taking** and **summarization,** and provide **sentence starters** to support note taking and writing for English learners; teach students to use **graphic organizers** and **illustrations** as a prewriting activity.

>> Beginning English learners complete Cloze sentences, early intermediate English learners complete a template of sentence starters and connecting words, and higher-level English learners complete templates with decreasing levels of writing support.

>> The teacher posts generic sentence starters throughout the classroom for easy reference by students.

Challenge students to expand their conceptual thinking vertically and horizontally: provide a range of resources, including **texts at different reading levels,** and have students use technology to research information and prepare presentations.

>> Students use texts and the Internet to expand their thinking and reasoning and to explore multidisciplinary connections.

>> Students use technology to create and deliver presentations.

Use as **assessment accommodations** — to support English learners in communicating what they have learned — the same strategies that support them in constructing new knowledge during instruction.

>> Accommodations such as graphic organizers, sentence frames, and oral cueing are assessment as well as instructional strategies that scaffold communication for English learners.

>> Students may select alternative ways (oral or written responses, multiple-choice tests, performance tasks) to demonstrate their understanding.

>> Both the teacher and students have frequent and varied opportunities to assess and monitor progress.

>> The teacher provides rubrics, models, and clear instructions for performance assessments.

ROCK CYCLE SCENARIO, GRADE 9

Starting from the first day of class, I work with my students to establish a classroom climate that is respectful and that allows them to feel safe to take the social and intellectual risks that are a necessary part of learning. I remind my native English speakers of our shared responsibility to encourage and engage students who are English learners.

In our community of science learners, I avoid the notion of "wrong" answers and focus with students on inquiries, hypotheses, conclusions, perceptions, opinions, and inferences. As I tell my students, it is the refinement of ideas and further questioning among the scientific community that advances scientific discovery.

In my mind's eye, the rock cycle sequence of lessons relates to future lessons that will establish deeper connections to the role of physics in the Earth's magnetic field, the reversal of magnetic poles, time scales, earthquakes and volcanism (differentiation of molecular structures of lava flows and types of eruptions), and how all of these relate to plate tectonics.

Two graphics (see below) serve as touchstones throughout the lessons: an illustration matching one in the textbook of the Earth's structure as a sphere with its interior layers, and an illustration of the rock cycle that students will annotate as we work through the lessons. This conceptual organizer graphic helps students relate rock materials and the processes that form them to plate tectonics as well as to make connections to the other spheres (hydrosphere, biosphere, and atmosphere).

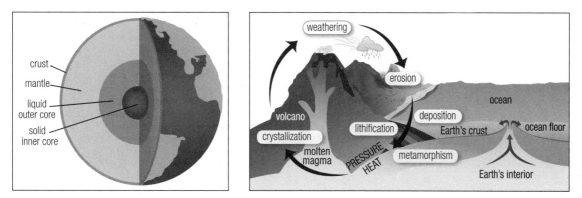

I also share with students the key standards that we will address, along with the essential questions we will try to answer.

Engage

During the engage stage, to gain insight into my students' understanding of the Earth's dynamic systems, and to engage their interest in our topic of study, I give students opportunities to explore and share their prior knowledge and related experiences. I also introduce models for organizing concepts and recording information that students will refer to and build on throughout the lesson.

EXAMPLE 1: VOCABULARY SELF-RATING

Students begin with a quick **vocabulary self-rating** of their familiarity with key terms in the lesson. I make it a point to limit the vocabulary to no more than 10 new words per lesson. Some words will be introduced during the engage stage; other words are embedded in the explore stage and reinforced during the explain and elaborate stages.

After students do the individual self-rating exercise, I like to get a quick visual distribution of the class vocabulary needs. I sometimes ask for hand signals for selected words or I can have students quickly mark a chart-sized class version of the vocabulary self-rating sheet. Later, as I monitor groups while they work on tasks, I also check students' individual self-rating forms and consider which key words to emphasize during the lesson.

In this lesson, I see that many of my students know the term "cycle." However, when I ask what the word means, I discover that most of my English learners know how it relates to bicycles and motorcycles but not to a revolving system in science. So, to move students from the known to unknown meaning of "cycle," I show a spinning bicycle wheel as an analogy to the water and rock cycles in science.

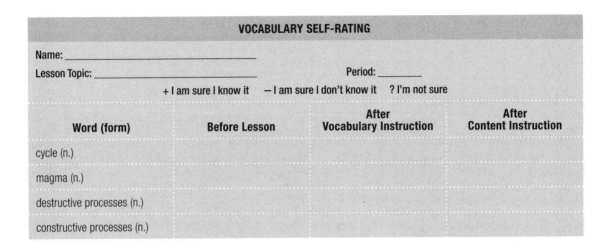

VOCABULARY SELF-RATING			
Name: _____			
Lesson Topic: _____		Period: _____	
+ I am sure I know it — I am sure I don't know it ? I'm not sure			
Word (form)	Before Lesson	After Vocabulary Instruction	After Content Instruction
cycle (n.)			
magma (n.)			
destructive processes (n.)			
constructive processes (n.)			

EXAMPLE 2: THINK-PAIR-SHARE AND KWL+

Now we prepare to learn about the interior structure of the Earth and its energy-driving mechanisms — in the context of rock formation. I show the touchstone **illustration** of the Earth as a sphere with interior layers to review its structure and introduce the idea of a dynamic and changing planet. This poster remains available throughout our lessons. Briefly, as a group, we identify each layer by name and brainstorm its key characteristics. (Later students will have the opportunity to research these concepts in more depth.)

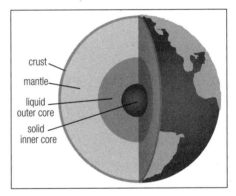

crust
mantle
liquid outer core
solid inner core

Next, I show **images** of volcanic eruptions and earthquakes[1] to engage my students and make connections to their prior knowledge and experiences. I ask, "What do you think makes a volcano erupt or an earthquake happen?"

With a partner, students **think-pair-share** and then share unique ideas with the whole class.

I record these in the K column of a **KWL+ chart** posted on the wall. As I record, I acknowledge students' contributions and reinforce their use of key vocabulary words.

Know	**W**ant to Know	**L**earned

EXAMPLE 3: CONCEPTUAL ORGANIZER GRAPHIC

At this point, I give each student a copy of the **conceptual organizer** graphic for the lessons — a diagram that they will annotate to show the rock cycle — representing another scale of the dynamics of our planet. We identify the labels for the landscape features, and I explain that students will be interpreting some of the Earth's transforming processes and adding labels as we go along. (I purposely do not identify the concept of the rock cycle since students will discover it on their own, making connections in deep ways that they can "own.")

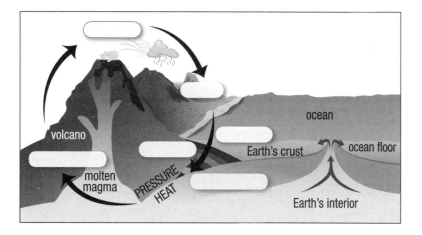

EXAMPLE 4: VISUALS AND MODELS

With the conceptual organizer, and drawing on students' prior explanations of volcanism, it becomes evident that volcanic materials may flow out of the sea floor as well as out of volcanoes.

To help students visualize and examine the rates of these transformations, I show a brief web-based **video clip** of erupting volcanoes on the sea floor. I demonstrate with a time-scale **paper model** the slow action of seafloor spreading and relate the rate at which the Atlantic sea floor grows as analogous to how fast a fingernail grows.

EXAMPLE 5: WORD WALL

I take this opportunity to write on the **word wall** two terms from the vocabulary self-rating, "constructive processes" and "destructive processes."

> constructive (adj.) processes Δ (n.)
> destructive (adj.) processes Δ (n.)

Next to "processes," I write the Greek delta (Δ) and tell students this is the symbol for change.

I explain that we are going to find out what they know about changes of the Earth and that we will learn more about these very important geologic change processes.

EXAMPLE 6: GLOSSARY

I distribute to groups of students sets of different **images** of natural disasters — volcanic eruptions, hurricanes, earthquakes, and floods — and explain the assignment, which is to sort the images into those that they think involve either destructive processes or constructive processes.

Since these are very complex concepts in geology, and at different scales they may be represented differently, I am aware that students' understanding will be gradual, building over the course of many other experiences and opportunities to engage with these concepts.

In debriefing, we discuss similarities and differences among the natural disasters, and as students describe the images, I begin on a transparency a T-bar **advance organizer** of key words. I ask students for definitions or to show illustrations of the terms.

On the transparency, I model this format as a **glossary** or **note-taking** strategy that students will continue to use, and I ask them to enter the words, their own definitions, and illustrations into a glossary that each will continue to build.

GLOSSARY / ADVANCE ORGANIZER / NOTE-TAKER	
Word / Term	**What It Means / Picture**
molten magma	very hot, melted rock
volcano	mountain made from molten rock coming from Earth's interior to the surface
Earth's interior	below the crust there are layers of solid and melted rock and metal

EXAMPLE 7: FORMATIVE ASSESSMENT

Referring to the conceptual organizer graphic, I conduct a quick **check for understanding**. Students use **hand signals** in answer to my questions and I note which concepts will be important to emphasize as we move into hands-on activities and group investigations during the explore stage.

I remind students that in both constructive and destructive processes change is taking place, and, as we learn more, they will build deeper, more academic understandings of these change processes. We formulate some questions for further research.

Summary: During the engage stage, I differentiated instruction for English learners in several ways:

>> I front-loaded certain new vocabulary terms and phrases.

>> I used established routines and familiar formats.

>> I controlled my speech, including by repeating and rephrasing, particularly for beginning and early intermediate level English learners.

>> I activated students' prior knowledge.

>> I provided meaningful context for new vocabulary and concepts.

>> I combined oral instruction with visuals (KWL+ chart, pictures, graphic organizers, demonstrations, models, and other resources).

>> I used think-pair-share and small group learning activities for a low-risk climate and to allow students to speak in pairs using English or their primary language.

Explore

My objective in the explore stage is to have students understand the concept that characteristics of rocks reveal their origin and to shed light on the kinds of transformations they might have undergone. I want students to begin relating these to geologic time scales.

As students identify common igneous, sedimentary, and metamorphic rocks, they will examine the processes that formed them. They will explore the cause-effect relationship that exists between plate motion and the continuous recycling of rock material.

EXAMPLE 8: EXPANDED AND AMPLIFIED LANGUAGE

One way I scaffold oral interactions is by **expanding** and rephrasing statements, especially for my English learners. Rather than simplifying, I clarify by giving contextual clues and synonyms and by introducing alternative academic language structures that carry the same meaning as statements found in our science textbook.

When students will be reading challenging text, as in the example below, I analyze key sentences that may need amplification. A lot of conceptual information is packed into brief passages and I want to be sure students understand the science that is represented. I may show a transparency such as the one below (and provide English learners with a corresponding handout for their science notebooks) depicting the two versions of the content, so it is visually displayed and students become familiar with this format. As part of reading the statements aloud, I may use a **think aloud** approach to make explicit for students how I make sense of what I am reading. I also support the text with images, explorations, and group discussion as needed.

As shown in the last amplified statement below, I also consider how these concepts relate to the learning experiences I need to plan. For example, students have some prior knowledge of what rocks are made of, but how, specifically, they were formed will be new knowledge, and where they were made will extend their new knowledge into connections with plate tectonics and time scales.

TEXTBOOK-LIKE LANGUAGE	TEACHER-EXPANDED / AMPLIFIED LANGUAGE
Rock's characteristics reveal their origin.	Rocks have characteristics that help us identify how they were formed.
These geologic processes yield three main types of rocks: igneous (volcanic origin), sedimentary (particle deposits or sea water mineral precipitates), and metamorphic (preexisting igneous, metamorphic, or sedimentary rock changed due to heat and/or pressure).	Every rock tells a story about the processes that formed it. Rocks can be igneous (from molten rock), sedimentary (particles settling out of water or mineral deposits), or metamorphic (any rock type changed due to heat and/or pressure).
Different types of rocks have different mineral compositions. Their mineral content varies depending on the source and process that formed the rock.	Rocks look and feel different. These differences tell us – what they are made of (prior knowledge). – how they were made (new knowledge). – where they were made (extended new knowledge related to tectonics).

EXAMPLE 9: MATRIX / ADVANCE ORGANIZER

Earlier in the unit, students identified sample rocks as igneous, sedimentary, or metamorphic. I project a transparency of the conceptual organizer, showing where these types of rocks are formed, and students refer to their individual copies. This activity reviews information, which is especially valuable for English learners, and adds context for our record-keeping, experiments, or data interpretations. On the organizer, I point to the volcano section and the labels "molten magma" and "volcano," saying, "Earlier we observed characteristics of three types of rocks, speculated on their possible origins, and identified the names that scientists use to sort each type. Now we will use simulation models and research skills to understand key processes in the formation of these three types of rocks."

I ask students to look at the **matrix** or **advance organizer** that they completed when they examined the three rock samples. The blank column for "Formation Process" will be the subject of our next exploration. I explain that to figure out which formation process goes with which type of rock, groups will consider the three formation processes at the bottom of the advance organizer. I read aloud the three formation descriptions.

MATRIX / ADVANCE ORGANIZER			
Type of Rock	**Sample**	**Characteristics**	**Formation Process**
igneous	obsidian	shiny, black, like glass, smooth, sharp	
sedimentary	sandstone	sandy, rough, yellow, gritty	
metamorphic	gneiss	multicolored, mixed lines of dark and shine	

Formation Processes:

(a) cooling of magma and other volcanic products (gases and ash)

(b) rising of pressure, temperature

(c) compacting of sand, microscopic sea life skeletons, and chemical precipitates; or deposited materials or rock fragments cemented together

I direct groups to review the characteristics they observed and recorded earlier for each rock sample. Then I direct them to compare the description of formation and type of rock to the images on the conceptual organizer graphic and to predict and record what is the most probable origin of each rock, based on the evidence and information they have at this point.

I monitor group work and check for understanding afterward by filling in a transparency of the advance organizer with group choices. If groups have made different predictions, I fill in the different choices and alert students that we will learn more about the formation of rocks to determine what information is correct.

EXAMPLE 10: MODELS

To recreate the rapid cooling that turns molten lava into glasslike obsidian, I create a "volcanic mountain" with a wide (used) candle. I have put a skirt of aluminum foil around it with some ice underneath. I light the wick and once liquid wax pools in the top of the candle, I blow out the wick and tilt the candle, letting hot wax run onto the cooled aluminum foil.

As a **think-pair-share** activity, I ask partners to think about an analogy between the cooled wax and the formation of volcanic rock. I invite a few volunteers to explain their thinking.

I explain that because the cooling rate of magma varies, within the volcano and when it becomes lava on the Earth's surface, the molecular structure of the rocks that are formed also varies. To help students visualize how the molecular structure of molten magma changes from loosely connected moving molecules into a crystalline lattice pattern — generally resulting in larger crystal formations the slower the cooling process — I guide a small group of students to act out the process of crystallization. I also use a set of molecule model links to make a pattern resembling the process of crystallization.

I point out to students that within the Earth systems context, they are able to connect across disciplines to learn the meaning of crystallization as a physical change that takes place at the molecular level. We add the words "crystal," "crystallize," and "crystallization" to the **word wall**, as well as the word "igneous."

> crystal (n.)
> crystallize (v.)
> crystallization (n.)
> igneous (adj.)

EXAMPLE 11: EXPERIMENTATION SKILLS

I bridge from categorizing rocks by their characteristics and chemical compositions to our new context and next lesson. To emphasize experimentation skills, I facilitate a discussion about what would be needed to perform a valid experiment to compare crystal growth. A crystal-growing station is suggested. As a class, students decide to compare varying cooling gradients with the same type of solution (such as one made with epsom salts), to compare different solutions at the same temperature, and to consider time as a variable. I record their ideas for the next day's explorations, and students enter into their glossaries the terms for these variables with brief definitions and illustrations.

By the time we complete these crystal-growing explorations, students have drawn on models, examples, and experiments to identify crystallization, a process in the formation of igneous rocks. Further in-depth study of the chemical structure of rocks and other Earth materials will come later. I ask students to update their conceptual organizer graphics with the terms "crystallization" and "igneous."

We continue to explore other images of tectonics models with web and print materials at varied reading levels.

EXAMPLE 12: VOCABULARY THINK ALOUD

Often students know the common meaning of words such as "weather" but do not know the scientific meaning in the context of the lesson's content standards. So I check for understanding of "weather" in the context of the rock cycle. As I **think aloud,** I also draw quick pictures or show illustrations.

"When I hear the word 'weather,' it makes me think about rain, cold, temperatures, wind, snow, hurricanes, and thermometers. When I hear the word 'weather*ing*,' I think about the paint on a house being worn away by sunlight or chipped away by wind and rain, or about waves crashing against rocks and breaking them into pebbles and into sand. One kind of 'weather' has to do with changes in the atmosphere. Another kind of 'weather,' the verb, has to do with weathering — breaking up and wearing down land and rocks. 'Weathering' is caused by water, wind, temperature changes, ice, and/or chemicals."

I add "weathering" and the related verb to the **word wall**. Students enter the terms "weather" and "weathering," and their word forms and definitions into their glossaries, along with supporting examples or illustrations.

> weather (v.)
> weathering (n.)

I also provide a "weathering" activity with sugar cubes at one of the stations where students will work next.

EXAMPLE 13: STATIONS

I ask groups to work independently at stations around the room to explore the formation of sedimentary and metamorphic rocks. Critical thinking cards at each station guide students to use visuals, build models, discuss what they are observing, and answer questions.

At a sedimentary station, students have several sedimentary samples to analyze. They use a "lake in a jar" to identify the clastic sedimentation processes of "sorting" and "stratification." If resources and time allow, they form a precipitate to explore chemically produced sedimentary rocks, and they use a microscope to analyze diatomaceous formations.

At a computer station, preselected websites in a My Favorites folder and a range of resource books allow students to connect their prior knowledge of rock structures with their developing understanding of rock formation and to research metamorphic rock formation.

I move from group to group, modeling the use of key vocabulary words and academic language and providing **cues** to frame students' explorations.

In addition, I support the beginning and intermediate English learners and provide them with **differentiated note-taking templates** that allow them to respond to the same questions as the other students. My goal is for all students to understand the concepts represented by questions such as the following:

>> Why did the rocks settle at the bottom?

>> What settled at the top and why?

>> What does Earth do to materials like these to turn them into layered rock?

>> What type of rock forms when all the materials are cemented by pressure and the leaching of minerals?

>> Are all sedimentary rocks layered? Are all layered rocks sedimentary? Explain your answer, supported by evidence or examples.

>> Draw an illustration and describe what compaction is. What is cementation? What is sedimentation? What is a conglomerate?

>> When the entire process of sedimentation has finalized, a rock has undergone lithification. What are all the processes a rock from a volcanic mountain would go through in its lithification (to become a sedimentary rock)?

Summary: During the explore stage, I differentiated instruction for English learners in many ways:

>> I used established routines and familiar documents and presentation formats. For example, we added vocabulary words to the conceptual organizer and word wall, I repeated words in the context of demonstrating, and I helped students apply words as they investigated and shared ideas in their groups and in class discussions.

>> I pointed out function words on a wall chart under the headings "cause and effect" and "sequencing/ordering" that I expect students to use as they describe what they observe.

>> Students always had the opportunity to hear a word, see the word, see it as a picture or illustration, and observe it within the context of a process.

>> I restated students' discourse to more scientifically express concepts, while validating their contributions to the group or class discussion.

>> I controlled my speech and repeated/rephrased for beginning and early intermediate English learners.

>> I supported oral instruction and demonstration with models, differentiated print and Internet text, and provided hands-on activities.

>> I used think-pair-share to lower the risk of participation.

>> I used think aloud to clarify meaning.

EXAMPLE 14: VOCABULARY SELF-RATING

As we prepare for a new lesson, I introduce a new set of key vocabulary words (compaction, erosion, lithification) and students use another **vocabulary self-rating** sheet to indicate their familiarity with these terms. Then, with a quick show of **hand signals,** I am able to check for students' understanding and adjust my lesson accordingly.

VOCABULARY SELF-RATING			
Name:			
Lesson Topic:		Period:	
+ I am sure I know it − I am sure I don't know it ? I'm not sure			
Word (form)	Before Lesson	After Vocabulary Instruction	After Content Instruction
compaction (n.)			
erosion (n.)			
lithification (n.)			

Explain

In the explain stage, I help students connect and relate everything they are learning: data from the stations and demonstrations and key vocabulary and concepts that they have recorded in graphic organizers, charts, and notes.

Students explain how different scale evidence supports the cause and effect relationship between the rock cycle and plate tectonics. They identify samples of the three types of rocks and show on their conceptual organizers where they would most likely be formed.

EXAMPLE 15: DIFFERENTIATED NOTE-TAKING TEMPLATES

At this point, I say to the class, "Now you are going to organize all of the information from your graphic organizers, charts, and our discussions."

Students work in groups; early intermediate and intermediate English learners are assigned to groups with native English speakers and more-proficient English learners. I work at a table with the beginning English learners. All English learner students have differentiated note-taking templates, depending on their ELD level, to help them address the same content as the native English speakers. (If I had any advanced English learners, which I do not in this class, they would have the same prompts as native English speakers.)

As the samples below from differentiated note-taking templates demonstrate, English learners are expected to use the new academic vocabulary and are supported to make meaning (expected student answers at the earlier ELD levels appear in italics). A complete note-taking template at any given level would have many more sentences, of course, and would cover all three types of rocks.

SAMPLE ITEMS FROM DIFFERENTIATED NOTE-TAKING TEMPLATES	
Beginning	The hot, liquid material inside volcanoes is _molten_ _magma_. Rocks formed from volcanic material are _igneous_ rocks. Water, wind, and ice help to _erode / move_ broken-down rock material.
Early Intermediate	Depending on how fast lava cools, it may form _crystals_. The slower the cooling, the _larger the crystals_. Wind, chemicals, rain, and _ice_ change rocks by _wearing them down / chipping them / breaking them into small pieces / weathering them_.
Intermediate	The main difference between lava and molten magma is _its location. If it is melted rock below the Earth's surface, it is magma. Once it flows to the surface, it is lava_. When lava cools, it _hardens / it can form crystals / it can form different kinds of rocks / it can mix with other materials to form different rocks_. Weathering and erosion begin the process of _breaking and moving rock material to deposit it as sediment_.
Early Advanced	Igneous rocks are formed by . . . Sedimentary rocks are formed by . . . Metamorphic rocks are formed by . . .
Advanced	Describe the origins and characteristics of igneous, sedimentary, and metamorphic rocks:

EXAMPLE 16: MANIPULATIVE ORGANIZER

I distribute to the groups labeled rock samples, resource books, and unlabeled rock samples. I ask groups to observe and record characteristics of the unlabeled rocks, label them, and justify their decisions. I model with a **think aloud** how groups might use information in the resource books and the provided rock identifying charts.

I ask students to be sure they have each completed the conceptual organizer, making sure to include all rock materials, all formation processes, and all rock types.

For my early intermediate English learners, I provide oral support and a **note-taking template** with sentence starters for each formation process.

I work at a table with the beginning English learners to scaffold their oral responses and acknowledge their efforts to make meaning. Along with images of rocks and the real samples of rocks they have already studied, they have a **manipulative organizer** (see page 104) that includes a large piece of paper with three labeled columns, cutout arrows, and labeled shapes (that could also include illustrations) that they organize to represent the transformation processes that each type of rock material undergoes to form a different type of rock. This activity is yet another way to help them understand and complete their conceptual organizers.

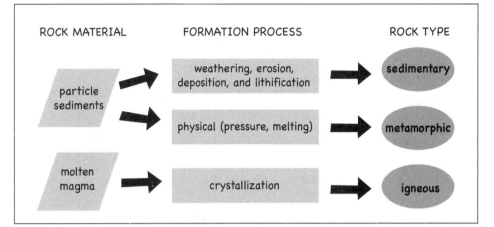

Summary: During the explain stage, I differentiated instruction for English learners in many ways:

>> I provided familiar routines and formats.

>> I reviewed with visuals.

>> I modeled and supported students to use academic language.

>> I used controlled speech and repeated and rephrased to clarify meaning for beginning and early intermediate English learners.

>> I used a think aloud to clarify meaning.

>> I provided reading materials at different levels.

>> I grouped students by ELD level for some activities.

>> I provided differentiated note-taking templates.

>> I provided a manipulative organizer.

Elaborate

In this stage, I review rock formation concepts and vocabulary with my beginning and early intermediate English learners. I help them expand their understanding horizontally by continuing to add context about the concepts that have been introduced. They may research and explain how one type of rock undergoes changes to become another type of rock and identify on the conceptual organizer where these changes would typically take place on our planet.

At the same time, the rest of the students elaborate their understandings vertically. They make cross-disciplinary connections as well as deepen their understanding of the physical properties of matter and the role of plate tectonics in our planet's ongoing changes. They may compare rock characteristics with those known from other planetary bodies in our solar system. They demonstrate their knowledge through projects such as presentations or web pages that explain or showcase the rock cycle for younger students at an elementary or middle school. They may begin to analyze chemical structures or properties of materials and their applications.

EXAMPLE 17: WORD WALL

In a table group of beginning and early intermediate English learners, I review the entries on the **word wall.** Students play a game involving the creation of showing sentences for words on the word wall, and I scaffold their use of academic language.

EXAMPLE 18: MANIPULATIVE ORGANIZER

I provide a **manipulative organizer** mainly to allow the beginning and early intermediate English learners to further review aspects of the rock cycle. However, this activity is also a valuable formative assessment tool for all my students. Depending on their level of English proficiency, students may organize vocabulary cards and arrows as shown below, including actual rock samples in the organizer; alternatively, given the labels, samples, and arrows, they may organize them in a way that depicts the most commonly known rock cycle transformations. Students may also manipulate the arrows to show how at any given point, the source material may undergo a different transformative process yielding a new product, which in turn may continue being recycled through other processes.

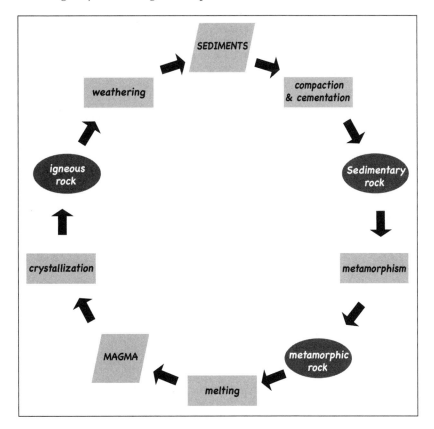

Evaluate

Throughout the lessons so far, I have checked for students' understanding, and I also embedded formative performance assessments. I make it a point to let my students know the purpose of a formative assessment — to ensure that I can do my best to help them learn. I provide multiple opportunities for students to demonstrate understanding, and I use the feedback to adjust my instruction to fit student needs.

When a summative assessment is scheduled, I let my students know in advance and explain its purpose — to evaluate their understanding of big ideas and to add to their course grade.

EXAMPLE 19: FINAL ASSESSMENT WITH ACCOMMODATIONS

I decided on the written summative assessment for these lessons when I began planning them so that I would have a clear vision of what proficient achievement should look like. I chose the textbook assessment and identified key words in the test directions and those required in answers to be sure that I taught and used those key words during instruction. I thought about accommodations that would make the assessment fair for my English learners, to enable them to show what they know about the science we have studied without being penalized for their level of English proficiency.

For the beginning and early intermediate English learners, I modify the assessment to include sentence frames. I also might need to read the test directions to the beginning English learners and otherwise provide oral scaffolding to help them complete the test.

When each early intermediate and intermediate English learner finishes the test, he or she brings it to me and I scan the answers for ambiguities. Then I can orally prompt to see if the student knows the answer but was unable to show it in writing.

EXAMPLE 20: PERFORMANCE ASSESSMENT

I give all students a performance assessment that involves creating a presentation about one of the rock formation processes. I work with the class to develop a **rubric** that will help guide their work. They understand that this is also the rubric that their peers and I will use to grade their presentation.

Each student receives a rock formation process "definition card" (see below). Depending on the definition, students select materials (from among those we have used in labs and demonstrations), design a way to explain and present the process, and then make an oral presentation to a group of their peers or to me.

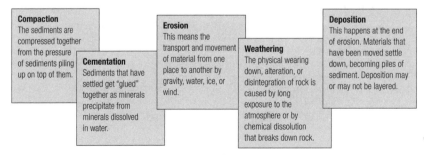

Compaction
The sediments are compressed together from the pressure of sediments piling up on top of them.

Cementation
Sediments that have settled get "glued" together as minerals precipitate from minerals dissolved in water.

Erosion
This means the transport and movement of material from one place to another by gravity, water, ice, or wind.

Weathering
The physical wearing down, alteration, or disintegration of rock is caused by long exposure to the atmosphere or by chemical dissolution that breaks down rock.

Deposition
This happens at the end of erosion. Materials that have been moved settle down, becoming piles of sediment. Deposition may or may not be layered.

If a student makes his or her presentation to other students, the group agrees on an assessment and submits it to me. I make the final grading decision. I also watch a sample of the presentations myself, perhaps those of specific students whose understanding of the unit I am concerned about or whose ELD level makes an oral presentation to peers too large a challenge.

For some English learners, student portfolios can be an alternative to the oral presentation. I provide a checklist of key entries and ask students to include summaries of our consultations and a piece of metacognitive writing that reflects on each student's learning process.

EXAMPLE 21: OTHER SUMMATIVE EVALUATION OPTIONS

I also have other ways to make summative assessments. I can review students' journal entries about discoveries they made throughout the unit. Their science notebooks can reveal how they gathered information and made use of charts, illustrations, or data. I can ask students to complete a research report showing expanded knowledge of a particular topic for display on our class website.

For my beginning levels of English learners, I can provide Cloze sentences and sentence frames to complete. I can give them exercises with familiar graphic organizers, such as an unlabeled conceptual organizer on which they position the types of rocks and tell a story about how a rock changed from one form to another.

Summary: During the evaluate stage, I differentiated summative assessment for English learners in various ways:

>> I embedded accommodations within the written assessments appropriate to each ELD level. For example, students could work with an unlabeled conceptual organizer, use illustrations to explain their ideas, and complete Cloze sentences and sentence frames. When I thought students' written work still did not represent their science understanding, I prompted them orally.

>> I offered choices, such as making an oral presentation to the teacher instead of to a peer group or, for more proficient English learners, completing a portfolio or research report instead of making an oral presentation.

SOIL SCENARIO, GRADE 6

Excerpts from lessons differentiated for English learners are described below in the voice of a grade 6 teacher as she conducts a series of lessons on soil composition and erosion.

She has identified key standards and essential questions, and has identified characteristics of her class composition and grouping.

Key National Science Education Standard

Grades 5–8 Content Standard D

Soil consists of weathered rocks and decomposed organic material from dead plants, animals, and bacteria. Soil is often found in layers, with each having a different chemical composition and texture.

Essential Questions

What is soil and how does it affect our lives?

What is erosion and how does it affect the Earth and our lives?

Class Composition and Grouping

In a class of 32 sixth graders, one-third are English learners, ranging from beginning to early advanced English proficiency levels. English learners are assigned to heterogeneous student groups based on language level (mix of ELD levels and native English speakers). Groups are seated around lab tables. Students in a group who have the same primary language are allowed to help each other understand concepts by using their primary language as necessary, but all students are taught and practice key science vocabulary words in English.

In these excerpts, I want to model some activities for teachers who are just starting to practice using differentiated lessons with English learners.[2] The intent is to show a few relatively easy ways to differentiate lessons. In this sixth grade classroom of 32 students, my English learners range across four proficiency levels, but for instruction I was able to collapse that to two levels (beginning and early intermediate are combined, as are intermediate and early advanced). The degree to which a teacher chooses to collapse levels depends on the demands of the class as a whole.

Included in these lesson excerpts are a number of examples that "zoom in" to show my actual verbal interactions with English learners at the two differentiated levels. The sample dialogues also show how to rephrase students' answers to model scientific discourse and academic language. This "scientific rephrasing" allows me to restate a student's answer to more closely approximate desired discourse. I also "control" the language that students must process by framing at least some questions and statements at the comprehension level of the English learners in the class. For example, I may pose a question to the whole class that is really meant for a beginning or early intermediate student to understand and have the opportunity to answer.

It is also valuable to notice how I combine verbal, visual, and hands-on instruction to create rich contexts that promote English learners' ability to comprehend science concepts. While talking, for example, I am often also showing, pointing, writing on wall charts or transparencies, or demonstrating a procedure.

Engage

In the engage stage, I want students to observe soil in their environment and think about their prior knowledge and experiences of soil as they brainstorm what they already know and want to learn. During this stage, I expand students' academic vocabulary and students build their understandings of key words.

EXAMPLE 1: GUIDED OBSERVATION

For this guided observation, I take the class outside and show students locations where gutters drain onto soil, grass, and cement. I use **guiding questions** to help students as they observe and compare the effects of water erosion. In the dialogues below, my questions and comments (T) are differentiated in the left column for beginning (B) and early intermediate (EI) students. In the right column, I am interacting with students at the intermediate (I) and early advanced (EA) levels.

GUIDED OBSERVATION: TWO DIFFERENTIATED DIALOGUES	
B/EI ELD-Level English Learners	**I/EA ELD-Level English Learners**
T: (Pointing) What is a <u>gutter</u>?	T: How is a gutter used?
EI: It is the thing on the side of the roof.	I: To catch rainwater.
T: Yes, a gutter is on the <u>edge</u> of a roof. It looks like a pipe or a tube that is open at the top (drawing a diagram and pointing to the roof).	T: Yes, a gutter is used to <u>collect</u> rainwater from a roof.
T: Does the water coming down hit soil or cement?	T: Where does the water in the gutter go?
B1: Soil.	I: It goes down to the ground.
B2: Cement.	T: How does it get to the ground?
T: (Pointing) The water hits soil here. The water hits cement over there.	I: Oh, it goes through the downspout.
T: Does the water <u>change</u> the soil here?	T: So, rainwater on a roof <u>flows</u> into a gutter. Then the water <u>flows</u> through a downspout to the ground.
B: Yes.	T: What <u>effect</u> does the water coming down have on the soil and cement?
EI: The water mix with the dirt and it make mud.	I: It hits dirt and make a hole there.
T: Yes, water mixes with dirt here and makes mud or muddy water.	EA: But over there it hit cement that has like a U-shape and the water flow to that big pipe with a cover on it.
	T: Yes, it hits the cement and flows down to the large underground pipe.

With the class still outdoors, I **model** collecting soil on a piece of transparent tape at three different sites where the soil is sandy, clay, or loam. I **read aloud** the student record sheet (see below) and ask volunteers to supply some sample answers. Then I give pairs of students a copy of the record sheet and ask them to collect samples of the three kinds of soil and complete the record sheet.

RECORD SHEET

Name _____   Name _____

Tape soil here

Location (Found)

This soil was found near the _____ .

This soil was found next to _____ .

This soil was found in the _____ .

This soil was found on the _____ .

Tape soil here

Location (Found)

This soil was found near the _____ .

This soil was found next to _____ .

This soil was found in the _____ .

This soil was found on the _____ .

Tape soil here

Location (Found)

This soil was found near the _____ .

This soil was found next to _____ .

This soil was found in the _____ .

This soil was found on the _____ .

EXAMPLE 3: KWL+ CHART

Back indoors, I use a KWL+ chart to record what students already know (K) about soils, what they want to learn (W), and, near the end of the lesson, what they have learned (L), and how these all relate (+).

To start, I ask students to brainstorm with a partner ideas about what they already know in a quick **think-pair-share.** I give partners about two minutes before I call on them and record unique ideas on our class chart, using **scientific rephrasing** as appropriate. I like to underline important vocabulary words and ask students for or provide a synonym that I write under each underlined word. At a later time, I transfer key words to the word wall. Following is an example of my students' ideas about what they already know about soils.

SOILS		
Know	**W**ant to know	**Learned**
There are different kinds of soils.		
It <u>absorbs</u> the water. (soaks)		
The soil has <u>nutrients</u>. (food for plants)		
It can have rocks and other things in it.		
It is used for growing plants.		
It is the top layer of the Earth.		
It is used for making different things.		

Next, I ask students what they want to know about soils, modeling with questions such as "What is soil?" and "Why is soil important?" Again, partners brainstorm for one or two minutes and I record unique ideas from the partners and use **scientific rephrasing** as appropriate. Following is the KWL+ chart with a sample of my students' questions.

SOILS		
Know	**W**ant to know	**Learned**
There are different kinds of soils.	What is soil made of?	
It <u>absorbs</u> the water. (soaks up)	Is sand a kind of soil? Is dirt soil?	
The soil has <u>nutrients</u>. (food for plants)	How does soil make things grow?	
It can have rocks and other things in it.	How old is soil? How did it get here?	
It is used for growing plants.	How does soil absorb water?	
It is the top layer of the Earth.	Can soil hurt us? Does it have germs?	
It is used to make different things.		

EXAMPLE 4: ENHANCED WORD WALL

On an **enhanced word wall**, I collect the new vocabulary from the KWL+ chart and add other words that are important in the lesson. I identify the difficult or abstract words that will need a **showing sentence.** Then I assign subsets of the words to student teams. For their assigned words, I ask each team to identify the word forms (confirming them with a dictionary), create beginning definitions (these may be informal; they become more sophisticated over time), and write any needed showing sentences. I also invite teams to paste or draw illustrations on the word wall. Below is an example of an enhanced word wall with my English learners' sample definitions and completed show sentences at two differentiated levels.

ENHANCED WORD WALL			
Word (form)	**Beginning Definition**	**Illustration**	**Showing Sentence**
flow (v.)	water moving in a stream		(B/EI) When water flows down...*it hits the dirt.* (I/EA) When water flows down...*it clears the path.*
cause (n.)	the reason something happens		(B/EI) The cause of the plants' good health is...*rain, sun, and no insects.* (I/EA) The cause of the plants' good health is...*enough rain, sun, and nutrients and protection from insects.*
effect (n.)	what has changed because of something else		(B/EI) When it rained, the effect was...*good for plants.* (I/EA) When it rained, the effect was...*to make the plants grow.*

Explore

During the explore stage, I have students investigate characteristics of soils and record their findings in terms of what they saw, felt, or smelled. I then ask students to categorize their describing words according to student-generated types.

EXAMPLE 5: MODELING A PROCEDURE

For each team of four, I prepare small plastic bags, labeled X, Y, or Z, of each of the three types of soil. I also provide each team with three index cards, a pad of small sticky notes, and two or more magnifying lenses. Students have copies of the lab directions on page 113.

To **model** each step of the soil investigation procedure, I show a transparency like the one labeled "Soil Observation Procedure" on page 114. I walk students through the four illustrated steps.

TEAM LAB DIRECTIONS

Step 1: Team Preparation

1. **Label** the three index cards X, Y, and Z.

2. Put a **pinch** of soil on each card. The soil should match the letter of the card. Soil from bag X goes on card X, etc.

Steps 2 and 3: Individual Observation and Writing

3. **Observe** soil sample X with a magnifying lens.

4. **Think to yourself** what the soil sample looks like.

5. Each team member write at least one "looks like" or visual **describing** word on a sticky note and put it on the index card.

6. **Feel** the soil sample.

7. Each team member write at least one "feels like" **describing** word on a sticky note and put it on the index card.

8. **Smell** the soil sample. (*Reminder:* To smell the soil safely, use your hand to waft air over the sample and into your nose (do not stick your nose close to the soil).

9. Each team member write at least one "smells like" **describing** word on a sticky note and put it on the index card.

10. Repeat with soil Y and soil Z.

Step 4: Team Sharing and Comparing

11. Share and compare all the describing words on each index card. What do you notice?

12. Compare the describing words on the different cards. What do you notice?

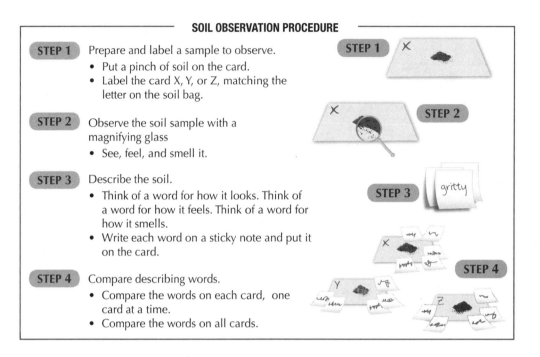

SOIL OBSERVATION PROCEDURE

STEP 1 Prepare and label a sample to observe.
- Put a pinch of soil on the card.
- Label the card X, Y, or Z, matching the letter on the soil bag.

STEP 2 Observe the soil sample with a magnifying glass
- See, feel, and smell it.

STEP 3 Describe the soil.
- Think of a word for how it looks. Think of a word for how it feels. Think of a word for how it smells.
- Write each word on a sticky note and put it on the card.

STEP 4 Compare describing words.
- Compare the words on each card, one card at a time.
- Compare the words on all cards.

EXAMPLE 6: QUESTIONS TO GUIDE STUDENT THINKING

As students work in their groups, I talk with them and, as necessary, guide their thinking. In the two examples on page 115, the left column shows a dialogue I might have with beginning and early intermediate ELD students. In the right column, the dialogue is differentiated for intermediate and early advanced ELD students.

GUIDED QUESTIONING: TWO DIFFERENTIATED DIALOGUES	
B/EI ELD-Level English Learners	**I/EA ELD-Level English Learners**
T: Are all soils the same?	T: Do all the soil samples look like the same material?
B: No.	I1: Y is mostly brown but there are little black spots.
T: What does your X soil look like?	I2: Z looks like it has little rocks and dirt.
B: Yellow.	T: It looks like it has different <u>particles</u> — some rock particles and some soil particles. We call these different parts "particles" (writes on the word wall).
T: Yes, your X soil looks yellow.	
T: Think of a word that tells how your sample feels.	EA: My X sample is sand. It is light brown so I think it has the same particles. It looks like there is glass in it.
EI: X is sand and it feels rough.	
T: Let's put <u>rough</u> on the word wall (for B learners).	T: It is a crystal.
T: In your Y soil, do you see small pieces or big pieces — small particles or big particles?	EA: Is crystal a particle?
	T: Yes, some sands do have crystal particles.
B: Small.	T: Is there a word for how sand feels?
EI: Tiny.	EA: It feels grainy.
T: Yes, your Y soil has small or tiny particles.	T: Let's put <u>grainy</u> on the word wall.
T: What would be a word to tell how it smells?	
B: Bad.	
T: What kind of smell?	
B: Like garbage.	
T: It smells bad like garbage.	

In preparation for the next part of the explore stage, I give each group a large piece of paper, a pad of sticky notes like those they already used, and several larger sticky notes of a different color. Then I model each step in producing a more complex chart of soil characteristics.

I keep my students in small groups so that English learners can hear and practice language in a "safe space." In particular, they will be repeating and rephrasing the directions that I model and thinking aloud about the charts they are building with their teams. As groups work, I continue to monitor and guide teams, coach English learners, and ensure that English learners are participating in meaningful ways.

EXAMPLE 7: HIERARCHICAL CONCEPT ORGANIZER

I remind students that they made observations about how their soil samples smelled, looked, and felt and already have a collection of describing words that they have shared with their group members. I repeat some of their examples, such as yellow, grainy, rough. I explain that scientists would call these *characteristics* of soil (I write the word "characteristics" on the word wall).

I ask teams to put all the characteristics they already wrote anywhere on the team's large piece of paper. I explain that teams will brainstorm many more characteristics of soil — as many words as they can think of that tell about the soil samples or ways to compare them — and will share ideas in a round-robin fashion so that everyone gets an equal chance to offer ideas. After each student gives an idea, the student writes it on a small sticky note and adds it to the team paper.

When teams conclude their brainstorms, I ask them to organize all their sticky notes into groups of characteristics that they decide go together. I **model** with one team's paper, rearranging a few sticky notes and explaining why they go together without giving them a category label.

Then I ask teams to think of a *category* name for each of their groups, explaining that the category is the word that tells someone why these characteristics are grouped together. I ask teams to write each category name on one of the larger sticky notes and arrange them where they each belong on the team's paper. I model with one team's paper the process of deciding on a category name — color, for example, writing it on a large sticky note, and placing it correctly on the paper. While teams complete the task, I monitor and help them rephrase category names to build academic vocabulary. For example, I suggest "texture" for "how it feels," "composition" for "stuff in it," or "particle size" to enhance "size."

Typically teams arrange their sticky notes in columns of characteristics headed by a category name as shown at right. Others may use varying organizing structures, but all identify their group categories. I capitalize on the variations in organization to highlight divergent thinking while pointing out the rational decision making that is key to all the solutions.

Explain

In the explain stage of this set of lessons, I want teams to create notes in the form of a matrix for three types of soils (as rows) and characteristics (as columns). English learners can complete this note-taking task because it involves logically arranging and adding words, not writing sentences.

EXAMPLE 8: NOTE-TAKING MATRIX

Before I ask students to create categories based on soil characteristics, I model the note-taking and categorization process by using a topic familiar to all students. With different samples of candy, I ask the class to help me sort them by type (chocolate bars, gummy candy, hard candy), and to name characteristics (e.g., rectangular, round, cylindrical) and categories of characteristics (e.g., shape). On a transparency, I demonstrate creating a matrix with types of candy and characteristics of candy (organized by categories).

I give a blank note-taking template for soil characteristics to each team member and give each team one extra copy. On a transparency of the template, I record all the headings of the matrix, including the names of the three types of soil (sand, clay, and loam), and the four categories of characteristics (color, texture, particle size, and composition) that students will investigate. If the concept of "composition" has not been addressed by any of the teams, I introduce the concept and enter the new word on the word wall. I invite volunteers to provide answers for a few of the cells. I explain that teams can have more than one characteristic in a cell and direct teams to complete the matrix using known words (from previous activities) and new words they might brainstorm.

TYPES OF SOIL	CATEGORIES AND CHARACTERISTICS			
	Color	Texture	Particle Size	Composition
Sand			large	
Clay		smooth, slippery		
Loam	brown, dark			dirt and plant parts

I return the soil samples and magnifying lenses to the teams, and ask teams to work together and complete one note-taking template for the team. I monitor teams and, after checking that the team template is correct, ask each member of the team to make a copy. Below is an example of a completed template.

TYPES OF SOIL	CATEGORIES AND CHARACTERISTICS			
	Color	Texture	Particle Size	Composition
Sand	yellowish white	rough, grainy	large	rocks and crystals
Clay	reddish tan	smooth, slippery	tiny, like powder	all the same
Loam	brown, dark	crumbly	medium	dirt and plant parts

Elaborate

Now, in the elaborate stage, I ask students to use what they have learned about soil characteristics.

EXAMPLE 9: PREDICTION

I ask students to make predictions about good uses for different kinds of soil. I ask them to individually fill in the prediction lab sheet shown below. They will perform a lab activity later to confirm their predictions. I can also use this activity as a check for applied understanding. If it reveals that I need to form a group of beginning and early intermediate English learners, I can do so and scaffold the activity with them as other students work independently on this assignment.

PREDICTION LAB SHEET		
Soil X — Sand	**Soil Y — Clay**	**Soil Z — Loam**
Texture		
Particle Size		
Which soil would be good for planting? X Y Z		
Because the soil… _____		
Which soil would be good for making a walking path? X Y Z		
Because the soil… _____		
Which soil would be good for making bricks or bowls? X Y Z		
Because the soil… _____		

Explore

In a return to the explore stage, I ask students to complete a hands-on activity to investigate soil porosity.

(Remember that the 5 Es do not always follow a unidirectional sequence; a teacher might move back and forth between stages for a variety of reasons.)

EXAMPLE 10: LAB DIRECTIONS

In a prelude, I make sure my English learners can understand the lab directions. In addition to providing each student with a copy of the directions shown below, I project a transparency of the student handout. The simple, step-by-step directions are supported by illustrations of the lab equipment required in each step. As I read each step, I use real equipment to show what students will do in that step. As a rule of thumb, beginning English learners can follow one-step directions in English, early intermediate students can follow two-step directions, and intermediate English learners can follow multistep directions with some support such as visuals and demonstrations.

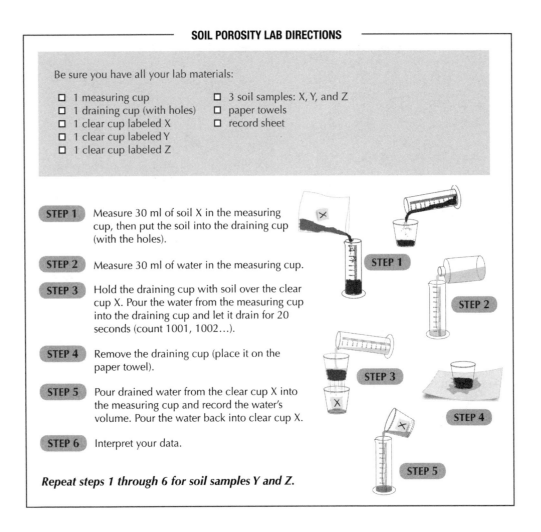

SOIL POROSITY LAB DIRECTIONS

Be sure you have all your lab materials:

- ☐ 1 measuring cup
- ☐ 1 draining cup (with holes)
- ☐ 1 clear cup labeled X
- ☐ 1 clear cup labeled Y
- ☐ 1 clear cup labeled Z

- ☐ 3 soil samples: X, Y, and Z
- ☐ paper towels
- ☐ record sheet

STEP 1 Measure 30 ml of soil X in the measuring cup, then put the soil into the draining cup (with the holes).

STEP 2 Measure 30 ml of water in the measuring cup.

STEP 3 Hold the draining cup with soil over the clear cup X. Pour the water from the measuring cup into the draining cup and let it drain for 20 seconds (count 1001, 1002…).

STEP 4 Remove the draining cup (place it on the paper towel).

STEP 5 Pour drained water from the clear cup X into the measuring cup and record the water's volume. Pour the water back into clear cup X.

STEP 6 Interpret your data.

Repeat steps 1 through 6 for soil samples Y and Z.

EXAMPLE 11: LAB EXPLORATION

I group English learners according to language level. I want to be able to guide both groups through the procedure and help students think critically at each step. An example of dialogue between the teacher and English learners is shown below.

GUIDED EXPLORATION: TWO DIFFERENTIATED DIALOGUES	
B/EI ELD-Level English Learners	**I/EA ELD-Level English Learners**
T: Which cup is used to measure water? Which cup is used to measure soil?	T: What is happening with soil X? Y? Z?
T: Which cup will hold the soil? Which cup will water go through?	T: Did soil X? Y? Z? drain the most or least?
T: Which cup is to collect the water that <u>drains</u>?	T: Why do you think the soils drained differently?
T: Which soil lets the <u>most</u> water through (gestures)? Which soil lets the <u>least</u> water through (gestures)?	T: What characteristics of the soil do you think made the most difference — texture, particle size, color, or composition? Why do you think so?
T: What makes the water drain <u>more</u> (gestures) or <u>less</u> (gestures)? Is it because of the color of the soil? Because of the size of the particles? Because of the texture? Because of the composition — what it is made of?	T: What evidence from your data supports your choice?

EXAMPLE 12: DIFFERENTIATED READING

In this excerpt from the elaborate stage, I provide reading assignments at three difficulty (readability) levels to increase access for English learners as well as for native English speakers who are struggling readers. One assignment is in the science textbook, and others are from a magazine and a trade book. I also assign an Internet website that has vivid pictures interspersed with text at the three reading levels. The various texts cover the same topic, sometimes with overlapping information and sometimes with related ideas that students can bring together in a group.

I assign students to heterogeneous groups of six based on ELD level and literacy skills. In each group, pairs of students have different reading assignments. In this classroom, because I have worked with students so that they respect each other as diverse learners, they feel comfortable with this type of leveled reading activity.

I model a **think aloud,** reading a short article as students follow along with their own copies. I encourage partners to help each other do this same kind of thinking aloud when they need to figure out something they are reading.

As partners read their assignment in soft voices together, helping each other with difficult words and concepts, I move around the room, monitoring especially pairs that may need more intensive reading support.

EXAMPLE 13: KWL+ CHART

Within each group, pairs share key ideas and a student recorder writes the pair's ideas on chart paper. When the partners all have some ideas recorded, I ask groups to share their charts with the class. Together we look for similarities and any unique ideas. Students' written ideas are rephrased as necessary to represent good models of academic language, and I transfer their ideas to the "L" column of the KWL+ chart to show what has been learned. I ask students to copy this information into their notebooks. I draw lines to connect the ideas in each column that are related, so that students recognize how they build understanding. At a later date, when I assign a summative assessment, these notes will help students review.

Evaluate

When I evaluate my students in formative ways, I make sure to use whole group responses, such as white boards and hand signals, to get a sense of where my students are with regard to a specific concept. For summative assessments, I make sure the format and questions align with the instructional models and graphics used during the earlier stages of my lesson. English learners benefit from having structures and formats in assessment that match those used to present information during instruction. They can focus on the assessment content if they do not also have to struggle to understand a new structure or format.

ENDNOTES FOR CHAPTER 7

[1] Such images are available at http://www.gesource.ac.uk/hazards/Storms-Educational.html.

[2] Marie Clark McEntee (teacher at Sylvandale Middle School, Franklin McKinley School District, San Jose, CA) contributed to the design of these lesson excerpts.

About the Authors

JOHN W. CARR develops resources and conducts workshops for teachers and teacher-leaders about practical approaches to standards-based classroom instruction and assessment for English learners. He makes presentations nationwide and consults with states on the development and review of English language proficiency standards and their application in classrooms. He developed the bestselling *Map of Standards for English Learners* and coauthored *The Bottom-Up Simple Approach to School Accountability and Improvement*. He has contributed to refereed journals and other education publications and has taught university courses in statistics, survey research methodology, and educational program evaluation at the University of San Francisco and Chiang Mai University, Thailand. He has a BA in psychology and an MA in research psychology from California State University, Sacramento, and a PhD in measurement, evaluation, and research methodology in education from the University of California, Berkeley. John is Senior Research Associate for the Evaluation Research program at WestEd. He may be reached at WestEd's Oakland, California, office or by email: jcarr@WestEd.org.

URSULA M. SEXTON conducts research and manages projects that investigate the roles that cultural diversity and language play in mathematics and science assessment development, testing, and instructional practices. She also contributes to projects involving teacher accreditation, school reform, systemic professional development, science and mathematics curriculum, access of academic content for English learners, and the use of technology in education. She is an advisor, presenter, and writer for state, national, and international science education projects and organizations. She contributes to science education journals and teacher textbooks, and she serves as editor and advisor of children's science books and education modules. She has served on federal and state science education panels and as a reviewer of National Science Foundation programs. As a former bilingual/science teacher and teacher educator, she has represented the profession as the 1994 California Presidential Awardee for Excellence in Mathematics and Science Teaching, the 1998 National Science Teacher of the Year, and the 1999 California State University–Hayward Teacher of the Year. She holds a BA in biological sciences from Holy Names College, and a multiple subject teaching credential with bilingual emphasis (Spanish) and a life science K–8 certification from California State University, Hayward. Ursula is Senior Research Associate for the Culture and Language in Education project and the Mathematics, Science, and Technology program at WestEd. She may be reached at WestEd's Oakland, California, office or by email: usexton@WestEd.org.

RACHEL LAGUNOFF contributes to the development, review, and alignment of state standards and assessments, with special emphasis on English language development, secondary level language arts, and adult English as a second language. She is coauthor with John Carr of the bestselling *Map of Standards for English Learners.* Her primary areas of interest are second language acquisition and language learning and use in education. She has taught university courses in linguistics, applied linguistics, and English as a second language. She received an MA in teaching English as a second language and a PhD in applied linguistics, both from the University of California, Los Angeles. Rachel is Senior Research Associate for the Assessment and Standards Development Services program at WestEd. She may be reached at WestEd's San Francisco office or by email: rlaguno@WestEd.org.

Free Reports Available from WestEd

Ensuring That No Child Is Left Behind
How Are Student Health Risks & Resilience Related to the Academic Progress of Schools?

Public schools are under enormous pressure to demonstrate academic gains on "high-stakes" standardized achievement tests. However, too many students come to school with developmental and health-related problems that make successful learning difficult, if not impossible. Schools seeking to improve student academic performance cannot ignore the role that health, school safety, caring relationships in the school, low rates of alcohol and other drug use, nutrition, and exercise play in their overall efforts. Based on data from the California Healthy Kids Survey administered by WestEd throughout the state, this report underscores the importance to academic achievement of key risk and youth development factors. According to this report, policies and practices that focus exclusively on raising test scores, while ignoring the comprehensive health needs of students, are likely to leave many children behind. A corresponding PowerPoint presentation is available that includes talking points and background information to enable anyone to make a presentation on the study results. To download your free PDF report, visit www.WestEd.org/cs/we/view/rs/740.

Thomas L. Hanson, Gregory Austin, & June Lee-Bayha
Order #: HD-04-02
Free PDF download available at www.WestEd.org/products (Hardcopies available for purchase)

Bridging Cultures in Our Schools
New Approaches That Work (Knowledge Brief)

"Teachers who serve each day as cultural mediators know the challenge goes beyond language. Even as they try to help immigrant students navigate a new system of education, their own teaching methods and most routine classroom expectations can come into perplexing conflict with children's cultural ways of knowing and behaving." — from the text

This Knowledge Brief provides a framework for understanding how teachers' culturally driven — and often unconsciously held — values influence classroom practice and expectations, and, when in conflict with the values of immigrant and other parents from more collectivistic societies, can interfere with parent-teacher communication. The brief looks at some specific sources of cross-culture conflicts and illustrates some strategies for resolving them. To download your free PDF report, visit www.WestEd.org/cs/we/view/rs/81.

Bridging Cultures Between Home and School Institute professional development is also available. Please contact Noelle Caskey at 415.615.3178 or ncaskey@WestEd.org.

Elise Trumbull, Carrie Rothstein-Fisch, & Patricia M. Greenfield
Order #: LCD-99-01
Free PDF download available at www.WestEd.org/products (Hardcopies available for purchase)

To find information on our research and services, or to sign up for WestEd's monthly E-Bulletin newsletter and other free reports, visit WestEd.org. To order call toll-free at 888-C-WESTED [888.293.7833]. To order online, visitWestEd.org/products.

Also Available from WestEd

Resiliency
What We Have Learned

Bonnie Bernard
$21.95
Trade paper
ISBN: 978-0-914409-18-2

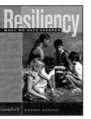

Ten years ago, resiliency theory was relatively new to the fields of prevention and education. Today, it is at the heart of hundreds of school and community programs that recognize in all young people the capacity to lead healthy, successful lives. The key, as Benard reports in this synthesis of a decade and more of resiliency research, is the role that families, schools, and communities play in supporting, and not undermining, this biological drive for normal human development. Of special interest is the evidence that resiliency prevails in most cases by far — even in extreme situations, such as those caused by poverty, troubled families, and violent neighborhoods.

An understanding of this developmental wisdom and the supporting research, Benard argues, must be integrated into adults' vision for the youth they work with and communicated to young people themselves. Benard's analysis of how best to incorporate research findings to support young people is both realistic and inspirational. It is an easy-to-read discussion of what the research has found along with descriptions of what application of the research looks like in our most successful efforts to support young people.

The Map of Standards for English Learners
Grades 6–12, Fifth Edition

**John Carr &
Rachel Lagunoff**
$12.95
Binder-ready
ISBN: 978-0-914409-29-8

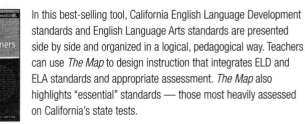

In this best-selling tool, California English Language Development standards and English Language Arts standards are presented side by side and organized in a logical, pedagogical way. Teachers can use *The Map* to design instruction that integrates ELD and ELA standards and appropriate assessment. *The Map* also highlights "essential" standards — those most heavily assessed on California's state tests.

To find information on our research and services, or to sign up for WestEd's monthly E-Bulletin newsletter and other free reports, visit WestEd.org. To order call toll-free at 888-C-WESTED [888.293.7833]. To order online, visit WestEd.org/products.